The hypnotherapist's companion

By Debbie Waller

 978-1-9998671-3-3 The hypnotherapist's companion

Published by Ann Jaloba Publishing, copyright © Ann Jaloba Publishing

DEDICATION

I completed this book during the Coronavirus lockdowns, when we all learned to re-focus on our goals, extend our comfort zones, and appreciate the support we get from family even more than usual. So this one is for Rachel, who will also one day write books. For Katharine, who will own the biggest library ever (and fill it). For Mum, who learned to Skype. And, especially, and always, for David: my sounding board, cheering squad, and the love of my life.

ACKNOWLEDGMENTS

A huge number of people have contributed to this work, knowingly and otherwise, and I offer them my grateful thanks.

'Otherwise' includes all those who have published studies, articles and research that helped me answer your questions. Also, my students, supervisees, graduates and supervisors who have challenged me to break out of my comfort zone, and my clients who are a never-ending source of inspiration when things get challenging.

Ann Jaloba, who helped me see how the various parts of this book could come together. Those who read through my early drafts and offered encouraging and constructive feedback: especially Brian Turner, Kathleen Roberts, Christine Howson and Joanne Ainley. William and Georgina Broom from the GHR (General

Hypnotherapy Register) and Sarah Whitaker from the NCH (National Council for Hypnotherapy) for their patience with my queries and their insight on a number of issues. And, last but never least, my husband, David, whose contribution was not just diagrams, but also being prepared to listen whenever I needed it as I worked out my ideas.

Debbie

CONTENTS

Foreword

Over the many years that I have been a counsellor, psychotherapist, hypnotherapist and coach I have read too many books to remember. Therein lies a problem, most of them were very similar. Few of them stood out, they were not memorable.

Then Debbie's book *The Hypnotherapist's Companion: a practical guide to practice* arrived in an email. My thoughts were: "Here we go again, another rehash of the same old stuff".

WOW! Did I get that wrong? I'll answer that rhetorical question for you. Yes I did, by a country mile.

I frequently do not bother to read introductions of books, but I decided to do so in this case and my education started right there. I was gripped by the concept of the acronym T.H.E.R.A.P.Y. In all my years of working in this field I had never heard of this and it is absolutely brilliant. Debbie explains it so perfectly as she has a style of writing that is easy to follow and visualise in the mind's eye.

From this point on, I went on to re-learning information and techniques I had forgotten. But much more importantly I was learning new ways of looking at hypnotherapy and of conducting sessions. I am not going to pick out specific chapters or other snippets of information. This book takes you through everything that you need to know to be a very competent hypnotherapist.

The major difference to other books, is how Debbie makes everything flow and fit together easily. Her style allows the brain to absorb the therapy information without the reader realising how much is being retained!

Debbie's breadth of knowledge and experience has created an incredibly easy to read source of knowledge for all hypnotherapists. It should be used by complete newbies right up to old hacks like me.

In her wonderful book Debbie has reintroduced me two valuable truths:

1. There are always new and original works being published to learn from.
2. Keeping up your CPD is extremely valuable, no matter how long you have been a hypnotherapist.

Dr. Richard Wain: Fellow and Membership Secretary of the Accredited Counsellors, Coaches, Psychotherapists and Hypnotherapists (ACCPH).

About the Author

I became a hypnotherapist in 2003, pretty much by accident and shortly after completing my degree as a mature student (students get better with age, like cheese). I found myself in a position of having lots of education, but no saleable skills. I had left school without any idea of what I wanted to do with my life and ended up in a fairly routine office job. Having taken time off to look after the kids and get the degree, I wanted to do something more meaningful.

I was looking for training that would enable me to employ myself, and my husband suggested attending the open day of a local hypnotherapy school. I went with no prior knowledge or experience, got hooked and the rest, as they say, is history.

Since then hypnotherapy has been my only career, though I'm still learning more every day and have added related skills such as stress management, a form of EMDR known as the BLAST technique, and coaching. I've worked part-time and full-time, as my family commitments allowed, and loved every minute. My clients are the most wonderful people, facing their situations with such courage and commitment that I am overcome with admiration. Who wouldn't want a job like that?

As well working as a therapist, I am a hypnotherapy trainer and supervisor. I'm a member of various professional bodies, and I was editor of the NCH *Hypnotherapy Journal* for three years. That is a lot of different roles but it keeps life interesting and I think that, whatever else I do, it's essential to be working regularly with clients if you are training and supervising therapists. Besides which, it's what I do.

I established Yorkshire Hypnotherapy Training in 2011, after several years of teaching for other training providers. The school has developed an excellent reputation, and I am very proud of its many graduates now in practice.

I've always been into books, and planned from childhood to be an author (though I thought then that I would write a blockbuster novel). As it turned out, life led me elsewhere and my first foray into authorship was becoming a contributor to *The Hypnotherapy Handbook*, an anthology of articles by experienced hypnotherapists and others. My first solo book, *Their Worlds, Your Words*, was published in 2016 and this is my second solo book.

The Hypnotherapist's Companion was initially inspired by my blog, published as the online magazine *Hypnotherapy Training and Practitioner*. Articles there are generally triggered by things I am asked as a trainer and supervisor, and I wanted to take that concept further. The current volume aims both to address the questions posed to me by those who are training and newly qualified and, perhaps, to provide a handy guide for other trainers and supervisors who might be asked those same questions. You'll find a few of the most popular articles from the blog, updated and extended of course, and lots of brand new material which hasn't been published before.

When we chose the title, I couldn't help thinking of Daphne Du Maurier's nameless heroine in Rebecca, who suggested that a companion is, "a friend of the bosom". I'm not sure where that leaves you regarding this book, so perhaps will go with a more useful definition. According to the Cambridge Dictionary it's, "someone or something you spend a lot of time with or travel with, or a friend who lives with you". I hope you will spend a lot of time with this book, whether you read it through or dip in and out, and that you will find it to be a useful friend.

Best wishes Debbie

Author's websites

https://yorkshirehypnotherapytraining.co.uk
Multi-Accredited Foundation and Practitioner level training in hypnotherapy, supervision for qualified hypnotherapists

https://cpd.expert
CPD opportunities for those who are already qualified as hypnotherapists and other therapy training

https://hypnotherapytrainingblog.blogspot.co.uk
Hypnotherapy Training and Practitioner, a free on-line magazine for hypnotherapists and hypnotherapy students

https://theirworlds-yourwords.co.uk/
Website supporting my first book

https://hypnotherapists-companion.co.uk
Website supporting the current volume, please see Appendix One for how to access the downloads.

http://www.debbiewaller.com
Hypnotherapy practice

Introduction . . .

but why are you telling me all this?

In the 1981 film *The Great Muppet Caper* the Muppets go to London to stop a jewel theft. Miss Piggy (of course) is amazing in her role as receptionist to a famous fashion designer; she is framed for the theft but cleared by Kermit and co. It's not the best Muppet movie ever, but it has its moments, one of which is when Miss Piggy has to listen to a long, complicated monologue by the designer (Diana Rigg) which pretty much sets up the rest of the film; plot, family history, goodies, baddies, everything.

"But why are you telling me all this?" she asks.

"It's plot exposition. It has to go somewhere," comes the deadpan reply.

As an author writing my second solo book (I previously also contributed to *The Hypnotherapy Handbook*, an anthology with several others) I had to decide how many references to the first one were too many. I'd like to think that some of you read *Their Worlds, Your Words*, but I know that not all of you will have done so, and there is nothing more annoying than an author constantly referring back to a work you haven't read. On the other hand, it's inevitable, since we're talking about related topics, that the odd mention will creep in here and there.

So I decided, a la Diana Rigg, the best option was to put what you needed to know upfront and plain to see rather than sneaking in references, footnotes or asides later on. If you've read the book, you can flick through these notes as a quick reminder. If not, it will tell you a few basics, and then we can move on. After all, it's plot exposition and it has to go somewhere.

In *Their Worlds, Your Words*, I talked about how to create effective and personalised session content for your clients, including how to adapt generic scripts to the person in front of you, and how to craft your own unique suggestions and metaphors based on what they tell you.

In the first section of the current work, The Therapy Loop, I'm going to look at how to extend these skills out of individual sessions and into creating a complete therapy plan based on your client's unique situation and goals.

I, therefore, think it would be useful to briefly introduce you to a couple of concepts from the other book: Brown's Question Cube and T.H.E.R.A.P.Y. If you want to know more, you'll have to read it, but this should give you enough to be going on with.

Brown's question cube*

Jacob Brown developed a system he called the Question Cube ('cube' because it is three-dimensional) for use by trainee therapists. These three dimensions are Orientation (whether the question is about the client or someone else), Format (how you structure the question), and Subject (what you are asking about).

The dimension we're most interested in to create a therapy plan is the one which deals with the subject of your questions. On this, Brown identifies five areas of interest, which are:

* Brown, J. E. (1997). The question cube: a model for developing question repertoire in training couple and family therapists. Journal of Marital and Family Therapy, 23(1), 27–40

- Behaviour, what the client does, has done and wants to do
- Feelings, what the client feels, has felt and wants to feel
- Beliefs, what the client believes or assumes that might impact on the therapy, for example, "smoking helps to reduce my stress."
- Meaning, clarifying words with vague or multiple meanings, for example, if the client says they want to feel "normal", what does that mean to them?
- Relationships, how does the status quo, and/or the proposed change, interact with other areas of the client's life or with the people who are important to them? For example, how does their partner respond to their desire to reduce their weight?

If these are the main areas we are interested in when collecting information from our clients, it stands to reason that they are also the areas we need to address in our therapy plan.

T.H.E.R.A.P.Y.**

This is an acronym which helps you to structure your client intake to ensure you have all the information you need. It stands for:

Test the goals

there are three tests to do before you agree on a goal:
(i) is the goal positive (i.e. something wanted)? if not, you should re-word it to be so.
(ii) is the goal SMART (specific, measurable, achievable,

** Waller, D., 2016. Their Worlds, Your Words: the hypnotherapist's guide to effective scripts and sessions. 1st ed. UK: Ann Jaloba Publishing.

relevant, time-bound)? if not, tweak it until it is.
(iii) does the goal need breaking up into smaller interim goals to be more manageable (chunking)? if so, (obviously) agree on the intermediate steps and deadlines with the client

History to here and now

This is just what it sounds like. When did the problem start? What has the progression been like? What makes things better, or worse? How do things stand now, especially in terms of Brown's five areas of interest?

Establish what needs to change

What specific changes would the client like to make?

Re-imagine the future

How will these changes affect the client and those around them? what will be different (again, consider Brown's five areas of interest)? What benefits will the client have gained? will they have lost anything they value now?

Add-ons and Aggravations

What will the client need to do, in addition to the therapy, to achieve these changes (homework, although we never call it this; see the article on that very topic later on, in the section on troubleshooting)? Can they think of anything likely to get in the way of progress?

Planning

Creating your session and therapy plans, and agreeing on them with the client

Yomp ahead

This is taken from Royal Marines slang for a march over

challenging terrain carrying full kit: in metaphorical therapy terms, shoulder the client's baggage and off you go. (I appreciate that one's a bit of a stretch but, in my defence, you're not exactly spoiled for choice when it comes to appropriate words beginning with Y.)

You don't need to approach every client intake in this order, of course. Some clients prefer to start with what they want the future to be like, others with how the past has been. Sometimes the goals aren't very precise until you've completed the initial interview. But if you cover all these areas sooner or later, you'll have a very comprehensive intake interview.

So that's your plot exposition, and on we go.

Section 1 – The therapy loop

(*developing flexible and effective therapy plans)*

Planning to be flexible

Stage 1: Information gathering and goal setting

Stage 2: Planning how to achieve the goals

Stage 3: Delivery of the therapy plan

Stage 4: Consolidation, learning and development for you and your client

Putting it all together: The Therapy Loop

Planning to be flexible

One of the most common questions I'm asked as a trainer is how to develop a therapy plan to move a client from a problematic here and now to the ideal future they imagine. This plan has to provide both structure, to guide the therapist, and flexibility, to allow for the client's changing circumstances. It needs to include the elements that are essential to a good result for client and therapist alike:

- Information gathering, and identifying the right goals and benefits
- Having an ongoing planning, review and selection process to identify the best techniques and scripts for the client
- Monitoring and measuring progress over time
- Consolidation to ensure learning and development for both client and therapist.

Having the right knowledge (such as rapport building, suitable techniques, motivational skills, and so on) is certainly a part of being able to plan your client's therapy. Unfortunately, even with this knowledge, you may still feel unsure about how everything fits together in a session or a series of sessions. That is exactly what I intend to address here.

One answer is to offer very structured programmes, so that every client with anxiety, or a wish to reduce their weight for example, gets exactly the same programme of sessions. That can work for some of the people, some of the time, but if you want to be truly effective as a therapist you need a more individual approach. This isn't just a cliché or assumption, by the way, there is evidence to support it. Nuland and Field (2020), for example, showed that smokers undergoing an "active, personalised approach" were far more likely to still be smoke-free after six months than those who were treated by a procedure that didn't include these elements (60% compared to 25%). (Nuland, *et al*, (1970)

It's therefore not my intention to give you the therapy version of a production line, or a session-by-session set of instructions. For one thing, this would undermine the whole purpose of my previous book, *Their Worlds, Your Words*, which was to encourage you to offer therapy which is imaginative, creative, and as individual as your clients.

Another reason for avoiding the production line approach is that everyone reading this book, will work in different ways. Some of you may like the cognitive approach, others may prefer to be more analytical. Each of you will know, and prefer to work with, different techniques.

What I do plan to do is to show you an adaptable outline which offers both flexibility and structure, so that anyone, no matter what their experience level or theoretical approach, can use it to make tangible progress.

The Therapy Loop maps how your client moves through your practice and helps you to remain focused on the right approach all the way. There are four stages, and we'll look at each one in detail first, then put the whole thing together into a flow chart that will guide you as you work with your clients.

Information gathering and explanations.
Measurement of pre-therapy status quo.
Identify and test the goals.
Prioritise if there are multiple goals.
Goal setting: ensuring that therapy can help
SMART, positive goals, chunked if necessary.
Specific motivators identified from re-imagined future.
Specific aggravations identified so they can be avoided or dealt with.

Stage 1: Information gathering and goal setting

This is where you will:

- Carry out your intake process to collect information about the client and what they want to change
- Check for contraindications or other reasons you might not be able to work with either the client or their presenting issue
- Explain hypnosis, the way you work, confidentiality, prices, cancellation policy, T&Cs etc.
- Agree on a way to measure the client's goals either objectively or subjectively. For a weight reduction client, this might be weight or dress size; for a client who wishes to reduce anxiety asking them to rate their anxiety on a scale of one to ten, or using a questionnaire such as the GAD 7* could be the best option. This is an important step because it will allow you to measure progress later on in the therapy
- Test that the client's goals are SMART (that is, specific, measurable, attainable, relevant, and time-bound) and positive, and decide if you need to break them into smaller steps before proceeding. If there are multiple goals, especially if they are unrelated, it's best to prioritise them, perhaps by asking the client to rank them in order of importance.

You can see from this list that the actions at this stage are generally a collaboration between you and the client. If a client's goal needs to be tweaked to make it SMART, for example, you would discuss the various elements and

* https://www.mdcalc.com/gad-7-general-anxiety-disorder-7

negotiate a final version of the goal which fits the bill.

You might complete the whole of this process with your client (online, in your therapy room or on the phone) or you may send them a form to complete in their own time. That's fine, whatever suits you and your clients is the right way to go. But before you go on to stage two, you should have at least the following:

- Confidence that you have the knowledge and experience to help this client
- Detailed information about the client's current situation and what they want to change, plus a thorough history of their issue
- The client's specific goals in a relevant format: that is, positive, SMART and divided up into manageable interim goals if necessary
- Knowledge of what motivates the client to make the changes they're proposing, and how they see those changes impacting on their life
- Some ideas about what the client thinks might get in the way of progress; for example, if they wish to quit smoking but have always given way to pressure from their friends to re-start in the past.

Once you have this, it's time to move on to stage two, and start to look at how you will use all this information to help the client reach their goals.

the therapy loop

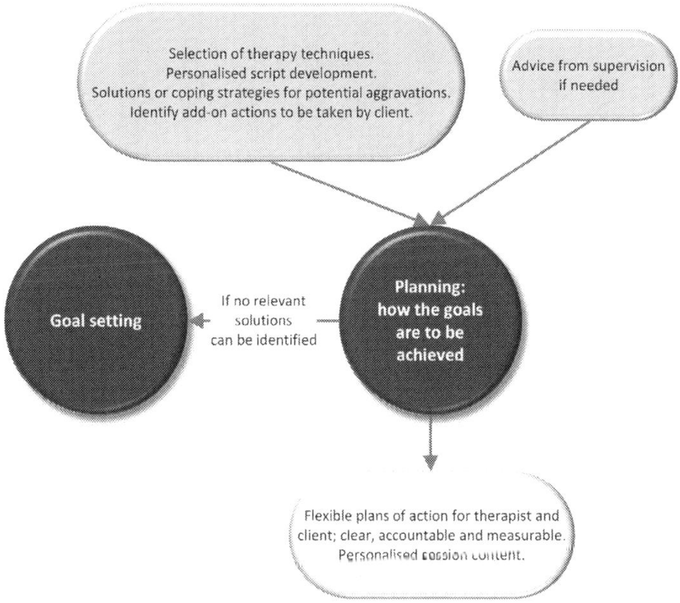

Stage 2: Planning how to achieve the goals

We're now at the stage of putting all the information we've gathered into a format that can be used to develop both individual sessions and an overall therapy plan.
The actions at this stage will involve:

- Agreeing on solutions or coping strategies for situations which can be anticipated, and which might otherwise slow or stop the progress of the therapy
- Agreeing relevant and practical 'add-on' actions to be taken by the client outside of the therapy sessions. For example; listening to an audio, practising a coping strategy, which you have discussed in therapy, in the

real world, or carrying out some action which tests the results of the therapy so far

- The therapist selecting or creating or adapting session content for the client which both creates movement towards the goal and supports the client's ability to use the new coping strategies and complete add-on tasks between sessions.

There is also, of course, the option to return to the goal-setting stage if necessary.

As most clients give you information in a conversational way, which might not be very structured, it's a good idea to break it down into its individual components*, then brainstorm the techniques and add-ons you know will be suitable for each element. I've done an example of this on the next page for a fictitious client, Joe, who has come to therapy because he wants to stop biting his nails. My entries, of course, have a lot less detail than if Joe was a real client, but they will do as examples.

* The components I've chosen for my chart are based on Brown's Question Cube and my T.H.E.R.A.P.Y. structure, so if you're one of those people who skips the Introduction of books, or reads them last, you might want to go back and look through the one in this book before continuing. It will outline these for you.

Therapy plan Pro-forma

Area of interest	History	Here and now	Re-imagined future	Aggravations	Actions and techniques	
					Therapist	Client
Behaviour	Started biting nails around age 15 during exams at school.	Bites nails and skin around nails. Avoids shaking hands when meeting clients at work.	Better stress management strategies e.g. deep breaths. Shake hands easily.	Doesn't always notice when he's doing it.		
Feelings	Has always felt ashamed of his nails, due to teasing in school	Anxiety and stress trigger behaviour. Feels calmer when he's doing it, ashamed if people notice his hands.	Calmer and more relaxed generally. Confident to show his hands. Proud of himself for reaching a goal.	Scared of failing again. he's tried to stop before.		
Beliefs	It helps reduce his stress levels	It helps reduce his stress levels. Fears other people are disgusted when they see his hands.	He needs to feel capable of making the change. Needs other coping strategies	Not sure he can cope without this habit.		
Meanings	Teasing means telling him girls wouldn't want him to touch them with his 'nasty hands'	Ashamed means he thinks people are judging him and looking down on him.	Success means he can be under stress without biting his nails.	Cope means feeling calm and relaxed under pressure.		
Relationships	Usually worse when he's stressed, especially when being judged, e.g. staff reviews, exams	Still stress-related, we could explore if it's also related to low confidence in social situations.	Associate stress with more positive coping strategies.	Staff reviews are coming up at work in the next month.		

This highlights patterns that you can explore within the therapy. Joe's reserve around others, for example, could indeed be due to worrying about what people think of his nails, but there may also be underlying social anxiety (perhaps relating to the teasing at school).

I've left the last two columns empty because what you put in there will depend on your theoretical orientation, what techniques you know and what type of add-ons you like to give your clients. If you tend to work analytically, for example, you might include regression to the age when Joe started to bite his nails. If you prefer a more cognitive approach you might ask him to keep a diary of when and where the nail-biting occurs. Either way, begin by brainstorming every script, approach or technique you know that might fit, then narrow them down to those you think would best suit Joe.

It's also worth noting that:

- At any point, the aggravations you enter into your plan can only be those which have happened in the past, or which you can reasonably predict; if others arise unexpectedly, like a family emergency or bereavement, you will need to add them to the chart and revise your plan accordingly
- Some techniques that you choose might come into more than one row, e.g. a control room metaphor or parts work could be used to effect change in more than one area, there's no problem with that
- You may not have entries in every box, especially in the client actions column
- If you are unable to identify any techniques to help with some aspects of the problem, you might have to go back to stage one, and revisit Joe's goals, bring this case to supervision, or perhaps consider referring him on.

Once you have a list of suitable approaches which, between them, address every element of the problem, you'll need to adapt them for Joe and arrange them in the order in which you'd like to use them. Again, this will be down to your individual preference, and whether you prefer to begin with the symptoms or the underlying issues. Don't forget to include the add-on tasks you'd like Joe to do between sessions.

Once complete, you have a clear plan of action for both yourself and your client, which specifies what each of you will do as therapy progresses. At which point it's time to move on to Stage 3, and start the therapy.

(A blank version of the therapy plan is one of the resources that can be downloaded from the book's website. See Appendix One for how to access these.)

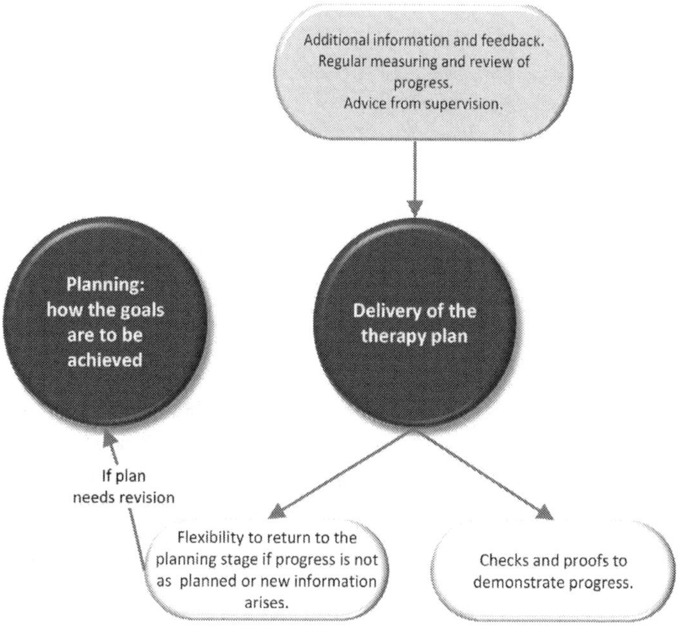

Stage 3: Delivery of the therapy plan:

This is probably the stage in which you will spend the longest time, as it's getting down to the nitty-gritty and putting your plan into action. Yomping ahead, if you like. What you put into each session, and the number of sessions you offer, will largely be dictated by your therapy plan, but you will rarely reach the end of it without some changes. There are several reasons for this:

- Clients sometimes reveal additional information as your rapport grows, or as they realise that something might be relevant
- As change happens, it can cause a ripple effect in the client's circumstances which either negates the need

for some approaches you had intended to use, or creates a need for different ones

- Unanticipated aggravations (barriers) may occur
- Progress may be generally slower (or faster) than anticipated.

As you can see from the diagram, to remain truly flexible there are various actions you need to take at this stage, in addition to providing therapy:

- Apply an on-going process of gathering information and feedback from the client. It can take careful questioning to identify some changes, especially those which take place gradually over a long time, or which feel very 'natural' from the client's point of view. I once had a weight reduction client tell me she hadn't noticed that she had been leaving food on her plate all week until a family member pointed out that, for her, this was very unusual behaviour!
- Undertake regular progress reviews, using any method which is compatible with the way you and the client agreed to measure success; for example, completing a diary or questionnaire, or asking the client to regularly rate their problem on a scale of one to ten. Reviewing at every session helps keep you flexible and responsive to the client's needs and prevents you from continuing an unsuccessful (or minimally successful) approach. Most reviews will naturally compare where the client is now with where they were in the previous session, but every so often it's useful to show how far they have come since the very beginning of therapy, as the incremental change is much larger. I'd advise doing this every three or four sessions
- Seek advice in a supervision session if it is needed.

As you carry these out, you may find that you move back and forth between the planning and delivery stages several times, but that's fine. New information or changes in circumstances can simply be integrated onto the therapy plan and solutions identified. There may be ideas from your original brainstorming which, although they didn't make it into the plan initially, now seem worth reconsidering, or you can look for new ones.

Once you and the client are confident that they are at or close to their goals, you can move to the fourth and final stage.

Stage 4: Consolidation — learning and development for you and your client

As therapy progresses successfully, your review process will eventually show that you have reached the client's goal. When that happens, some clients worry about ending therapy, perhaps because they have grown used to it, or because they wonder whether they will be able to maintain their gains alone. This is why you need a consolidation process to give them confidence, and deal with any concerns, as they end their work with you.

Once you agree that the client's goal has been met, check that their 're-imagined future' is what they expected it to be, now that they have it.

Ask:

- Does it offer the benefits they wanted? (If not, why not? Therapy may need to continue if there are more benefits to be realised.)
- Are there benefits to reaching their goal that they didn't expect? What are these?
- Are there other positive changes that seem unconnected with the goal? Therapy can create ripples that widen into different areas of the client's life, and many will report that they feel more confident, for example, or generally less stressed, even if these weren't anticipated when you started to work together.

You can also ask if the skills that you have taught them could be applied elsewhere in their lives; often coping strategies learned for one situation will generalise well to others. Realising this empowers your client, giving them a wonderful sense of wellbeing as they end their therapy.

Finally, in your last session, you can use techniques like future pacing to bring together all positive changes the client has reported (not just the successful goals). Encourage them to continue habits, such as setting aside time for themselves, that they have begun during your time together.

Although (quite rightly) our main focus is on the client and their goals, as a therapist you are also in a learning process and it's important to recognise this as therapy ends. Whether you have been in practice for two weeks or two decades, every client adds to your experience and skill level, and you need to be pro-active in making the most of it. Before you put away your client's records, have a good read through and make notes about:

- What you have learned, and what skills you have improved by working with this client
- What went to plan, and whether you now feel it could have been improved
- What didn't go as well as expected, why this might have been and how you might avoid the same thing happening again
- What went better than expected, why this might have been and how you can use this knowledge in the future
- Whether a need for further professional development has been identified by your work with this client, and if so where you can get it.

This is called reflective practice and we'll look in more detail at how to do it well later in this book.

You can also consider whether to take this client to supervision if you haven't already done so, which can help to give you a different perspective on some of the points above.

We have been building up a flow chart as we move through this process. There are a couple of boxes yet to add, and I think they are fairly self-explanatory. For clients, therapy can be a linear process or a circular one.

If their goal is met and no work remains to be done, they will exit the process. Sometimes, however, there were multiple goals from the outset, or new goals have been identified as the therapy progressed. If these have not yet been addressed, you will return to stage one and begin again, setting out the new goals, planning and delivering the therapy.

For therapists, therapy is always a circular process. What you learn (or are inspired to seek out) from each client

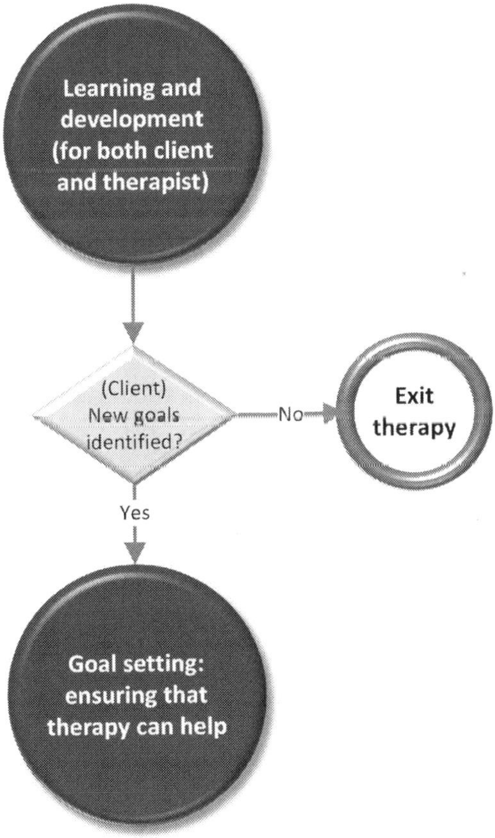

improves the services you offer others. Each time you go round the Therapy Loop you get better at what you do and your clients benefit. That can only be a good thing.

The diagram on page 37 brings together everything we have talked about and shows you the Therapy Loop in its entirety. It might look a bit complex at first glance, but look carefully — it's simply a combination of all the smaller diagrams we've used throughout this section, so you can go back to them if you prefer.

Putting it all together: The Therapy Loop

The most valuable aspect of using the Therapy Loop in your practice is not just that it allows you to plan, monitor, and review your therapy as you go — or even that you can be both structured and flexible in the way that you offer it. It's that it produces continuing benefits — to the client, of course, but also to you as a therapist, and to you as an individual.

By consistently reviewing and reflecting on our performance and achievements as therapists, and by being honest with ourselves as we do that, we all grow stronger and become more powerful in our ability to help others and ourselves.

This approach emphasises your learning, development, and personal and professional growth as a person as well as a professional offering therapy to clients. In effect, it offers a virtuous circle of self-reflection and improvement which will make you a more effective and adaptable therapist.

the therapy loop

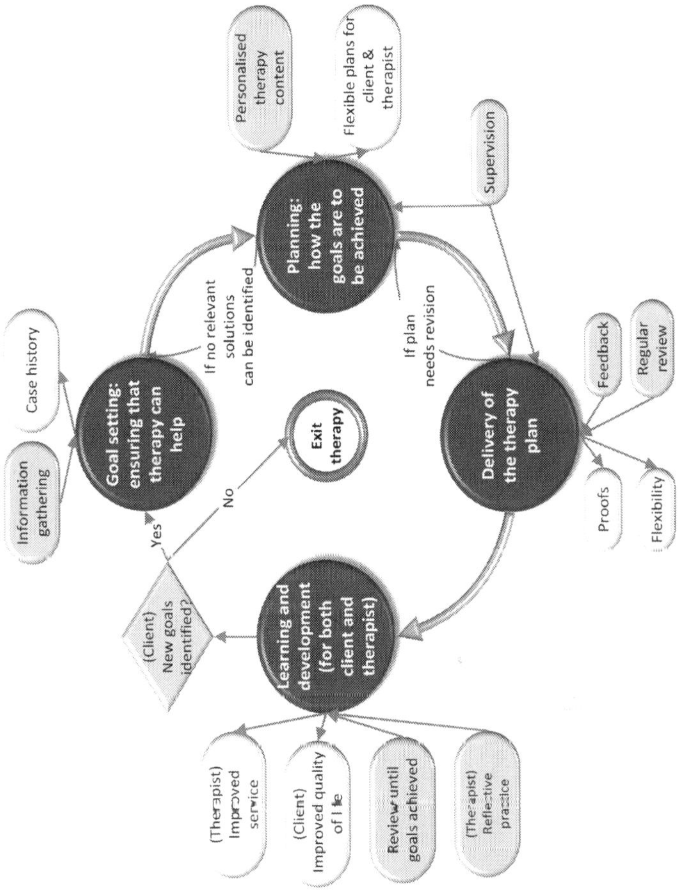

We've had to simplify the wording somewhat in the final diagram, so it's readable on an A5 page.
A full colour, A4, detailed version of the Therapy Loop is one of the resources that can be downloaded from the book's website. A blank version of the therapy plan is one of the resources that can be downloaded from the book's website.
See Appendix One for how to access these.

Section 2 – Developing your skills:

Managing client expectations

Using scripts properly (and when to let them go)

Working with non-visual clients

Using silence in therapy

The role of therapist self-disclosure

The effective use of aversion

Managing client expectations

In *First Steps: how to set up a therapy business and stay sane*, (2014) a book about setting up your hypnotherapy practice, Ann Jaloba says: "If I had a pound for every client who says, 'I don't expect magic', I would be rich. If I had a pound for every client who meant it, I would not." And I don't see how anyone could put that better.

You do, of course, get the one-session wonders where the client's whole life seems to change overnight, but I suspect that's at least partly because the client is completely ready to make that change. You were simply a catalyst, or perhaps provided a sense of separation between one set of behaviours and another. For most clients, improvement is an ongoing process rather than a one-off event; they want the change enough to have reached out for help, but achieving that state of 100% readiness is part of what you are working on together.

So, it's important to manage their expectations of therapy right from the start, whilst remaining upbeat and positive.

The best times for managing expectations seem to be either when a potential client first contacts you to make an appointment, or in the early part of the first session. Ekberg *et al* (2016) studied recorded therapy sessions to see how therapists approached this task and concluded that: "Clients may more readily engage from the outset of therapy when provided with an explanation that manages their expectation of what is involved. Therapists can accomplish this by projecting how therapy will proceed, particularly beyond the initial session."

Ekberg identified three patterns of managing client expectations in a first session.

1. Explain your plans for the first and later sessions early on in the therapeutic process, and gain the client's agreement. For example: "We'll probably work together over several sessions to help you get to where you want to be. The first one will be about getting to know you, finding out what's brought you here, and establishing your goals for therapy. Once we've done that, we can talk about how hypnotherapy can help you achieve those goals and put together a plan for future meetings. How does that sound? . . . Do you have any questions?"

2. Explain your plan for the first session only, this is said to be the most common approach. This, of course, has less risk of overloading your client with information, and also allows you to decide your long-term approach after you've spoken to them about their situation. For example: "In this first session, I'd like to get some information from you about what's brought you here today. I'm going to ask you some questions and if you don't understand why I'm asking something, feel free to ask me about it. It's your therapy and we'll be working together on finding some solutions. Have you any questions about that now?"

3. No explanations offered of what's involved in therapy. For example: "Hello, nice to meet you. Now, why don't we start with you talking about the kind of situations that are problematic for you at present?" This was the rarest of the approaches, used by only two of fifteen therapists in the study. It tended to be associated with a lack of engagement from clients, so the study does demonstrate the relative value of using some explanation.

Ekberg was looking at CBT sessions, but I think it's reasonable to assume that the principles generalise quite well to other kinds of therapy. As hypnotherapists, however, we have additional expectations to manage because of the myths and beliefs that clients might have come across about hypnosis itself. I tend to spend a few moments in each client's first session asking them if they have any knowledge or experience of hypnosis, and why they have chosen it to help them. It's an interesting opening to the session and gives you a chance to debunk some myths if you need to.

It's worth having a few answers ready for the most common misconceptions, a kind of therapeutic version of, 'here's one I prepared earlier'. Assuming the client has the right sense of humour, I used to say: "If it was mind control my kids would have tidy bedrooms".

Other areas where you might want to use expectation management include:

- When, why and how the client can contact you between sessions
- Tasks or activities they are expected to complete between sessions, and why these are important
- How often sessions will be held
- How many sessions you estimate the client might need, and how you will review this
- Timekeeping, cancelled sessions etc.

That's quite a lot of information to remember, so having it written down for your client to take away and refer to later is probably a good approach. But going through it briefly in the session ensures they know what's in the written material and have the opportunity to ask questions if they wish.

In fact, Ekberg (2014) showed that: "comprehensive expectation management was associated with clients remaining in therapy for 1.4 sessions longer than those who received no expectation management." So it's worthwhile taking some time for explanations, to help improve your client's understanding and willingness to continue therapy.

And, from a client satisfaction point of view, it's comforting to be able to see where therapy will take them, and how.

It's a win-win situation for both of you.

Using scripts properly, (and when to let them go)

I appreciate that hypnotic scripts are a controversial area, so I'm going to take a look at the pros and cons.

Arguments against using scripts:

- They can prevent you from having creative ideas of your own
- They distract you from observing the client or relating to them as individuals
- They don't reflect your clients' specific situations
- They are a prop for inadequate therapists with no ideas or skills of their own.

Arguments for using scripts:

- You never go blank in a session
- There is time to craft your hypnotic language perfectly, especially if you are inexperienced or not a naturally quick or creative thinker
- They can give you ideas for phrases, words and concepts that you might not have come up with yourself
- They are useful if the exact language you're using is important (for example, in confusional techniques), or you are using a metaphor about something the client loves but is unfamiliar to you (for example, computer games or golf)
- They give you an insight (at least when they are good scripts) of what the industry leaders say to their clients, why re-invent the wheel?

I think all the arguments against scripts have some merit and would never suggest that a couple of inductions and a book of scripts turns you into a hypnotherapist. But my theory is this: even experienced pilots use a checklist when flying a plane. No-one suggests it would be OK to leave someone to fly a plane with just the checklist and no other experience but, alongside proper training, they help.

It's just my view but I think, used in the same way, scripts have enough advantages to make them worthwhile, especially if you are a student, newly-qualified, or working with an issue for the first time.

I find it hard to believe that anyone could literally use 100% unique content for each person they work with. Our language is rich and varied, but there are only so many ways to give a message about quitting cigarettes or making healthy choices. So, I'm going to go out on a limb a little and say we probably all use scripts (or frameworks, protocols, or whatever else you want to call them), at least to some extent. It's just that some people have words written on a piece of paper and some draw more generally from ideas, words and phrases in their heads.

If they were called guides instead of scripts, I feel there might be fewer objections.

Using scripts as guides

If you want to know how to personalise scripts – where to break in and what to break in with – and how to create your own, original suggestions and session content, I suggest getting hold of a copy of my book, *Their Worlds, Your Words* which will take you through it step by step.

Broadly, though, I would look for places where a script is talking about Brown's five areas of interest – behaviour, feelings, beliefs, relationships, and meanings. Take out the generic descriptions and reflect your client's words and experiences.

Even before a client session you can go through your scripts, and mark these passages, so it's easy to know where to weave in your client's details when you have them in front of you. You can personalise scripts to yourself as well as the client, by which I mean re-write them so they sound like you. For example, the first relaxation script I was given included the phrase: "The muscles relaxing like a handful of loose elastic bands." I really hated that phrase – in my view, elastic bands are twangy, not soothing – and I substituted something else very quickly.

There may be words or phrases which don't feel natural to you, perhaps because the script's author is American and you are British (or vice versa), or because of your regional accent or dialect. Swap them about until you sound one hundred per cent comfortable when you read them aloud.

Always read through your scripts before a session, and preferably practise reading them aloud a few times. The more familiar you are with the content, the more natural you will sound.

Have I got a script for that?

Sometimes a very scary question.

One of the problems with scripts not directly covered in my pros and cons lists (though related to your ability to be creative) is that your client may turn up with an issue that you haven't got a script for, especially if you are newly-qualified and have limited experience of different issues. Or they just have an unusual situation. (One of my clients, for example, needed to swap from being right-handed to being left-handed for medical reasons. She kept forgetting and wanted help to make the switch.)

The answer is to get creative.

Have a few metaphors handy that can easily be made to suit whatever situation the client is in. The Control Room, for example, is a classic and very adaptable.

Ask the client to imagine being in a control room or looking at a control panel of some kind. This can be adapted to their interests so, if they like computers, have it look like a motherboard that needs rewiring. If they love the beach, place the control panel inside a beach hut. And so on.

Find the controls that deal with the client's issue, whatever that is, and adjust them accordingly. You can turn pretty much any feeling or behaviour up or down, depending on whether the client wants more of it or less. With my client, for example, I could have found the controls for 'handedness' and turned right-handed down or off, left-handed up. Then, before you count them out, do some future pacing incorporating the suggestion that the changes made in the control room will be reflected in the real world when the client leaves your clinic.

The session is not a placeholder while you get advice, but should have a real impact. And the joy of metaphors is that the client will make them into what they need to be, so they are very effective. Other techniques, like parts, swish, anchors, or regression adapt naturally to whatever the client is facing, you just need to get the right information to use them with.

But once you've done that, where else can you get inspiration?

How to have a script for everything

Given that I've advised you to use scripts as a source of ideas alongside your training, and not as a word-for-word text to read out exactly as they are written, there are many places you can get inspiration for session content. Then, all you have to do is use your skills to frame them into suitably hypnotic language:

- Use the scripts you do have more creatively in a kind of hypnotic pick-n-mix approach
- Combine ideas, phrases and concepts from several

different scripts in one session to get what you need for your client:

- Ignore what your scripts say they are about. Look for patterns and triggers that are similar to your client's situation rather than their literal problem. For example, a script for nail-biting may have ideas for hair twiddling; one for confidence in public speaking will adapt to anxiety about an oral exam; ideas from a social anxiety script may adapt to an upcoming interview
- There are blogs out there on any topic you care to name. Google 'tips on how to [do what your client wants to do]' and a million or more articles will come up. 'Tips on how to deal with presentation nerves' for example, gave me 17,600,000 hits. Read a few and they'll suggest coping strategies, positive affirmations and other useful information that you can adapt for your client
- Get your client to provide information you can use – for example, asking them to look at blogs and bring five relevant coping strategies they feel comfortable with to the next session; use their list as the basis of some personalised future pacing
- Self-help books, support groups, webinars and courses – unless your client's issue is very unusual, there will be resources like these around. Even though they're aimed at clients, not therapists, they will give you ideas and insight, and accessing them may count towards your CPD hours. Just be careful not to infringe the author's copyright, especially if they include worksheets!
- Your imagination – go with the flow and don't be afraid to go 'off-piste' even if you usually work with scripts. Metaphors, ideas and words that pop into your head during a session come from your unconscious mind; they are responses to what your client has said and may

use bits of information your conscious mind didn't fully notice. Trust your training.

Going script-free

I said earlier that 'scripts have enough advantages to make them worthwhile, especially if you are a student, newly-qualified, or working with an issue for the first time.' But what if you're none of those things? Or what if you just want to try striking out and 'doing your own thing'?

As Eleanor Roosevelt said, you should 'do one thing every day that scares you' and ditching the scripts can be something that stretches you as a therapist, keeps you on your toes and increases your personal and professional satisfaction.

My own first experience of going script-less was definitely scary. My therapy room at the time was above a kind of New Age shop; it sold dream catchers, tarot cards, crystals, you know the sort of thing. I booked in five clients a day (an hour each plus time to nip to the loo and write up notes in between) and you could almost guarantee that if anyone cancelled or failed to show it would be the middle one, leaving me with spare time but not enough to go home or do much that was useful.

One Saturday this is exactly what had happened, my middle client cancelled, so I was passing time chatting to the person at the till. One of my previous week's clients came in to let me know that, although she had been successful in quitting smoking, she was struggling at times and wanted to book in her 'safety net' session.

'That's OK,' said the shop assistant, 'She's had a cancellation, she could fit you in right now!'.

Oops.

I wasn't willing to admit that I couldn't do a session

without my scripts so off we went, and everything was fine. The client was happy, she got results and I realised that the scripts had become something I used by habit. They were on my lap, but I rarely looked at them and frequently didn't stick to them. So why bother?

You may find that you, too, come to this realisation over time, or you are pushed into it, as I was.

Perhaps your client turns up with a complete change of direction and the session you had planned – or the script you brought with you – is no longer appropriate.* Or perhaps you just want to give it a go, to develop your professional skills.

Here are my tips for getting inspired and gradually weaning yourself off scripts:

- Learn a few inductions by heart by all means, but remember that these too can be personalised
- Make sure you are familiar with the rules of hypnotic language, so you use them automatically when creating off the cuff suggestions
- Continue to read well-written scripts, for ideas, words and phrases that you can make your own in sessions. They will come to you when you need them, if you trust your own unconscious mind
- Get your favourite scripts down to bullet points at first, so you have something to refer to if you go blank but don't have a word-for-word outline
- You don't need to learn vast quantities of information by heart, but get the 'stories' of a few scripts, especially multi-purpose metaphors, in your memory so you can adapt them when needed

* Although, these days, having everything on a tablet is probably the way to go, since you can easily carry around your entire collection.

- Practise on family and friends to gain confidence that you can do this!

It may be weeks, months, or years after qualifying that you feel you can work without scripts. You might let them go before the end of your training, or you may never feel the need. Then again, maybe you're ready right now.

It's entirely your decision based on what you feel is right for you and your clients, but I'd say give it a go. You may surprise yourself.

Working with non-visual clients

About non-visualisation

The inability to visualise has a name, aphantasia, which is described as the inability to form mental images of objects that are not present. It's considered to be a neurological issue and MRI scans have shown that relevant areas of the brain are inactive or dormant in those who struggle with visualisation. Francis Galton talked about people who couldn't visualise as far back as 1880, but there was very little interest in it until a report by researchers at Exeter University (Zeman, Dewar and Della Sala, 2015) called "Living without Imagery", which also proposed the name 'aphantasia'. Zeman became interested in this area in 2010 after meeting a man who, having previously had the ability to visualise, lost it following coronary angioplasty .

When the report was published, several people came forward saying that, for them, this was a normal state of affairs; subsequent research confirmed that around 2% of us do, indeed, seem to have no 'mind's eye'. Zeman suggested that this was a condition similar to synaesthesia, in which people experience the world in unusual sensory ways, for example, musical notes or days of the week might have a definite colour or taste.

Zeman also found that aphantasia occurs on a spectrum. Within his non-visual group, he investigated both voluntary (deliberately trying to imagine in images) and involuntary (spontaneous images flashing into the mind) internal imagery and found:

- 9 out of 21 subjects reported substantial deficit in voluntary imagery
- 12 out of 21 subjects reported 'total' deficit in voluntary imagery

- 10 out of 21 subjects reported the occasional involuntary 'flash' image whilst awake
- 17 out of 21 subjects reported some degree of involuntary imagery in dreams.

He also reported that the people in this group had trouble with tasks that most people use visualisation to complete, such as answering, 'How many windows are there in your house?' I'm sure you can see that this was a very small-scale study and more work is needed, but at least it gives us some general guidelines.

Can aphantasia be 'cured'?

We tend to assume that everyone else thinks the same way we do, and many people don't realise they are aphantasic until something happens to show them that others think differently. Until then, they assume that other people's references to mental images are purely a figure of speech . Although his first experience of it was with someone who had lost a pre-existing ability to visualise, Zeman suggested that aphantasia is usually congenital (present from or before birth). Various discussions on aphantasia.com suggest that it can also be acquired by injury or trauma.

A quick online search will find you some suggested cures, including some hypnotic audios. Most seem to involve the repetition of visualisation exercises, and anecdotal evidence from those using them is that they help.

On the other hand, the only formal study I could find wasn't very promising. Shank and O'Dowell (2017), worked with a partially-aphantasic man, who could initially only visualise in dreams. He underwent eighteen weekly, one-hour 'vision therapy' sessions and also carried out visualisation exercises at home. By the end of all this, he reported that: "he had been able to visualize more [just] before he fell asleep but had not noticed any significant difference in his day-to-day life. Furthermore, none of the visual processing testing or the Vivid Imagery Questionnaire showed improvement in his scores."

Zeman says that although his original subject did eventually regain some of his ability, he believes that no one born with the condition has managed to learn to visualise. Some test subjects apparently report that they can do so under the influence of hallucinogenic drugs, but that's probably a bit drastic for most of us!

If congenital aphantasia is, indeed, a sign of an inbuilt difference in neurological connections from the norm then maybe a permanent 'cure' isn't possible although, for those who develop the condition via trauma or injury, re-eliciting past skills seems like more of a possibility. It depends, I suppose, on how you see the mind/body connection.

To be honest, for most of your aphantasic clients, their inability to visualise will not be the presenting problem, so whether you can cure the condition is not an issue. It's just one of those personal characteristics you have to bear in mind when working with them. Zeman agrees. He says: "It's an intriguing variation in human experience, not a disorder".

Aphantasia and therapy

We live in a visual-centric world. If you think about the fact that 98% of people visualise well and, of the remaining 2%, some visualise at least a bit, that seems fair enough. But it can be frustrating for those who don't have much of an inner eye to work with therapists who assume they do. Zeman (2015) said, "Sceptics could claim that aphantasia is itself a mere fantasy: describing our inner lives is difficult and undoubtedly liable to error," and there has been a tendency in some therapists to be dismissive of those who said they could not visualise. The most common responses I've come across are, 'Of course they do, they just don't recognise it' or, 'Ask them what colour their front door is; if they know they must be visualising'.

From the point of view of someone whose visualisation skills (even in dreams) are pretty much zero, I can tell you it doesn't work like that. I have a way of coding visual information, of course, but it isn't in pictures. I can move around an imaginary scene like a forest by 'sensing' what is there, like being in a familiar place in total darkness. I can also tell you what colour my front door is, but there's no mental image that goes with recalling it, more a kind of 'just knowing', combined with an auditory/verbal description.

(A quick digression here. My neighbour, a very visual person, once asked me 'If you don't visualise, how can you recognise a chair when you see it?'. Simple, it's the inner eye that doesn't work. Apart from a growing need for glasses as I get older, the outer ones work just fine, thank you.)

Essentially telling your client that they're wrong when they say they don't visualise isn't a very empathetic or client-centred approach, in my humble opinion, nor does it 'work with what a client is giving you'. As therapists, we can – and should – do better.

Aphantasia may limit some clients' ability to access certain types of therapy. Art Kavanaugh, who has aphantasia, highlights the number of therapeutic techniques which rely on positive visualisations of the present or the future, and wonders if this could cause therapy to be less effective for those unable to imagine in this way. (2018)

He asks if it is possible that the condition could make it harder to overcome anxiety, in that the aphantasic is unable to visualize favourable (or any) outcomes to possible actions, or alternative future scenarios? He also suggests that there could be a connection between the inability to visualise and the development of anxiety.

Might it not be the case that aphantasia, as well as hampering the management of anxiety, actually makes anxiety more likely in the first place? We all know that the future is unpredictable and beyond our control. And it seems obvious that uncertainty and a sense of not being in control are liable to cause anxiety. So it doesn't seem that much of a stretch to suppose that a capacity to picture possible futures might help to make the future seem more predictable and therefore less threatening. And, as a consequence, less likely to induce anxiety.

Kavanaugh is speaking from his own experience of undergoing therapy for anxiety, and Zeman's original (2015) study did show that aphantasia tended to affect relationships and mood.

Logically, Kavanagh's ideas could also be applied to other clients: those who wish to reduce their weight but can't 'see' themselves as slim, or those who can't 'see' themselves as non-smokers, for example. It can also be distressing for someone who has suffered a personal loss not to be able to picture the face of the person they are grieving for.

As therapists, we have to find a way forward that relies on other ways of processing information, when working with aphantasic clients. In order to do so, let's just stop for a minute and look at the name 'aphantasic'. Literally, it means an inability to fantasise; being 'without imagination', but this is misleading. Why? Because imagination and visualisation are not the same thing.

That's a big statement but it's the crux of the matter. I may not be able to 'see' a beach or forest inside my head if you ask me to, but I can certainly imagine being there, and so can your clients.

So, how can you help them do so?

- Accept what the client says about the way they think and reassure them you can work with it
- Get into their world and leave your own behind; don't assume you know better than they do how and what they are thinking
- Discover your client's strengths and use those in your sessions. If they're not good at thinking in pictures, how do they think? What's easy or effective for them?
- Remember that aphantasic clients may still give you visual metaphors when describing things, but they are purely a figure of speech and don't indicate literal visual images
- Watch your language: it does help if you use words like 'remember' or 'imagine' instead of 'see' or 'visualise'
- Zeman (2015) said that people with aphantasia often have trouble recalling autobiographical memory, presumably because they can't picture events or people in their past. If this is a problem for your client when you complete your intake form, give them a list of questions to take home, and encourage them to ask family members for help
- Ask your client what format they prefer information to be provided in. Mind maps, diagrams and other visual representations of information may not mean as much to someone with aphantasia. (My particular dislike is instruction videos; I just want a written list!)
- After the first trance experience, ask the client how they got on with potentially visual experiences like the 'peaceful place'. Remember that in the Zeman study, 80% of people with aphantasia reported a degree of involuntary visualisation in dreams and, in my personal experience, some find this also happens in hypnosis

- Avoid approaches and techniques which rely on complicated visual manipulation. For example, as we've said, the peaceful place is fine as long as you bring in all the senses and don't rely on visuals. The Rewind (Fast Phobia Cure) technique, which comes in a few different formats but typically requires the client to change images from colour to black and white, from a still image to a film, and to run the film backwards and forwards at different speeds, is likely to be too much. You could try adapting it (the sounds of the experience coming from a radio, instead of imagery) but, in my opinion, you are probably better to simply find a different approach
- People with aphantasia have the same emotional response to looking at photographs as anyone else. Use visual props so there is something physical to look at to help the client access their current feelings or the ones they want to have in the future. If you want them to access memories, they could be asked to bring in a photo of themselves at the right age
- Find ways to imagine a positive future or present that don't rely on visualisations – using kinaesthetic or olfactory (smell-based) triggers and anchors, for example.

It's standard advice to work with what the client gives you, and particularly important if the client struggles to visualise because it's something you may take for granted yourself. Build your rapport, step into the client's world, listen to their feedback and you will increase your ability to work with all clients, whether they have a clear inner eye or not.

If you feel you may be aphantasic, the Aphantasia Network has a test online at https://aphantasic.com/vviq

Using silence in therapy

We talk a lot about communication skills in therapy, but one which tends to take a back seat is silence. Not the kind of exaggerated silence you get from a mime, or even your partner when you've had a disagreement, but the different ways in which silence itself can be a form of communication between you and your client.

Silence as non-verbal communication

In most day-to-day situations, silence means the total absence of noise. In conversation, however (therapeutic or otherwise) it simply means the absence of speech. But the absence of speech doesn't mean there is an absence of communication.

One of the presuppositions of NLP is that 'you can't not communicate' . Potentially confusing double negative aside, this means if two people are together, they are communicating, even if no words are passing between them. The absence of words is a communication of its own; whether it's a comfortable 'together' kind of silence or an angry, defensive one.

Within therapy, silences may happen naturally as part of the ebb and flow of conversation, or you or the client may initiate them deliberately.

There is evidence to show that, for therapists, initiating silence can be a way of building rapport, especially early on in the therapeutic process. Sharpley, Munro and Elly (2010) said that: "significantly higher amounts of silence during [initial client interviews] rated as Very High in rapport versus those rated as Low in rapport" and that "counsellor-initiated but client-terminated silences were more likely to contribute towards rapport than silences that were initiated and terminated by the counsellor".

The advantage we have as hypnotherapists (over counsellors, psychotherapists etc) is that clients, and some therapists, tend to divide the session into two parts. There's the talking part and the therapy part, which is the hypnosis. The truth is, however, that our hypnotherapy will only be effective if we have the right level of rapport and the right information from the client, to begin with. The talking part is just as important as the hypnosis and including some counselling skills in your repertoire can boost your effectiveness as a hypnotherapist significantly.

So, for now, I'm focusing on the conversational part of your session, and we'll come to the hypnosis later.

Types of silence in therapy

First of all, it's fair to say that not all silences are golden. Lane, *et al* (2002) said that silence can, "deeply facilitate the therapeutic encounter" but also pointed out that: "If this intervention is not skilfully and sensitively employed by the practitioner, the client may feel the therapist's quietness as distance, disinterest, and disengagement, leading to breaches in the trust and safety of the therapeutic alliance."

Where silence indicates a problem

These first few points are where silence might indicate a problem in the session:

- Avoidance. Some clients may use silence to express their resistance to therapy, or their unwillingness to share information with you. This can be a real problem if someone is sent for therapy, perhaps by a parent, partner or employer, and doesn't want to be there
- Pushing the client too far, too fast. Silence may happen if your client is generally willing to engage in the therapy

but reluctant to share a specific piece of information at that moment

- Not coping. Silence might be an indication that the client is feeling overwhelmed; perhaps not yet ready to admit to or confront their feelings
- Not feeling listened to. Silence may be an indication that your client feels you don't understand what they're saying or disagrees with something you've said, but doesn't feel comfortable enough to challenge or correct you
- Fear of saying the wrong thing. Clients may feel that the only answer they can give to a question is too revealing, or confrontational, or that you will judge them for it
- Transference. The client may be transferring elements of another relationship, in which they were expected to be silent or not to express an opinion, into the therapeutic one.*

Where silence is useful

Other silences can be much more positive and helpful:

- Silence offered by the therapist. There is no therapeutic value in letting your eyes become unfocused as your

* I went into transference in some detail in 'Their Worlds, Your Words', so I don't intend to repeat that information here but, broadly, it's a concept from psycho-analytical therapy, in which a client takes their feelings about a person or object (in the original, usually a parent) and transfers them to something they perceive as similar (in this case, the therapist). So, if you remind the client of their Mum, for example, they will unconsciously respond to you as if you were their Mum. Counter transference, which will come up in a later article, is a similar process but in the other direction, when the therapist transfers some of their own preconceptions or experiences onto the client.

mind wanders to planning your holiday or wondering what to have for tea, leaving your client to feel that they might as well be alone in the room. It has to be comfortable, a time of relaxed waiting, in which you remain centred on the client, noting their non-verbal cues, such as changes in breathing, facial expression and body language.

- Self-reflection or moments of insight for clients. Clients may need to think about things you say, or even about hearing themselves expressing their feelings or situation aloud, perhaps in a particular way for the first time. If you rush in with your next question the moment, and perhaps the opportunity for healing, is lost
- Freedom to experience emotions. Silence can be a time-out for clients who are experiencing strong emotions, letting the natural progression of the feeling continue, without rushing on to the next point
- Thinking time for you. Don't be afraid to take some time to think about your next question, or where you want the conversation to go, especially if the client has just given you a lot of information in a huge chunk. Better to think how to phrase your response, using clean language, than to hurry to fill the gap and end up leading your client
- Asking for more information. Even the most comfortable silence has a natural rhythm and end. As you pause and wait, your client may add extra information without you needing to think of a question at all
- Being client-centred. Following on from the last point, silences let the client choose the direction of the conversation, and avoids you diverting their thoughts before they get to what's really important to them.

Responding to a silent client

The main question when the therapy room falls silent is whether to let the situation continue or to intervene. Your choice on this will probably depend upon which interpretation you put on the silence. If you feel the client needs some processing time, for example, you may be more disposed to just letting it happen than if you feel the client is avoiding an issue.

Given the numerous meanings and purposes that silence can have it's impossible to have a 'one size fits all' way of dealing with it. But you could consider the following:

- Just be with the client. Wait it out with patience and calmness, and don't allow wandering attention, frustration and other negative reactions to communicate non-verbally to the client
- Use behavioural and verbal mirroring to reflect the client's silence back to them
- Offer a brief observation such as, 'You seem quiet today'
- Repeat the client's last verbalisation as a question to prompt a further response, for example, "You don't know what to do?"
- Reassure the client that any information they share will be treated with respect and is confidential
- Ask the client about their silence, inviting them to put their interpretation on it, so that you can work with that
- Offer a change of subject and come back to the point later. Clients may not be ready to reveal all their secrets at the beginning of therapy; sometimes it takes a session or two for them to feel enough trust to share some things with you

In most circumstances, working on your rapport should help. Ensure you are focused on the client, using all your listening skills and letting them guide the conversation. The more at ease the client feels with you, the better the conversation is likely to flow.

Silence in hypnosis

Milton Erickson once had a very talkative client with a compulsion to comment on everything she noticed in the environment around her. He avoided interrupting her by silently drawing her attention to different objects in the room, polishing his glasses, for example, or moving an object on the desk. As she stopped her chatter to enquire about the indicated objects, her sense of anticipation grew, wondering what he would do next. He then associated a word or phrase with each object and eventually guided her into trance by asking her to recall the objects in turn and go deeper with each one. After a number of these meetings, she would enter trance whenever he pointed at the chair in which she sat for sessions.

You may or may not feel able to use silence in quite this way, but there are plenty of other options once you get to the stage of guiding your client into trance.

Techniques where the client is talking to you during trance, such as regression, have a natural conversational flow. You may need to be patient if the client's replies come slower than in waking conversation, but you can take your cue from them.

If you are using approaches which do not require the client to speak aloud, then you will have to observe and calibrate your client to ensure that they are doing what you've asked them to do.

For example, if you are using a relaxation sequence there is no point gabbling off: "Focus on your feet, relax all the muscles along the soles of your feet, over your feet, up through your ankles, calves, thighs and all the way to your hips . . ." as fast as you can.

Whilst the unconscious does seem to process information much faster than the conscious, no-one can relax, imagine a scene, or do much else, the instant it's out of your mouth. Without some silence to allow the client to do what you've asked them, you will leave them struggling to keep up.

Try building in some silences for processing time, and ask the client to let you know, via an ideo-motor response or nod of the head, when they've done what you asked. You'll find some respond quicker than others, but asking for feedback of this kind and waiting in silence till you have it will enable you to work at exactly the right speed for each client.

Silence can also be a great way of deepening a trance. Consider this:

Now I want you to count backwards from 100 inside your head, silently, with your thoughts. Just silently counting backwards. 100 . . . 99 . . . 98 . . . [saying the numbers slowly] . . .

and, as you count, you'll find yourself going deeper and deeper into trance . . .

deeper and deeper with every number . . .

[long silence]

and the strange thing is that the more you count, the more you relax, and the more you relax, the deeper you go . . .

and the deeper you go the less the numbers matter . . .

until, eventually, you'll find your own perfect level of trance and stop counting . . .

[long silence]

and when you're there, at your own, perfect level of trance, just let go of the numbers and allow your unconscious mind to give me a nod to let me know you're there.

And then you wait it out while the client takes themselves to where they need to be. Simple, completely client-centred, and perfect timing for every client.

Of course, you could always make it even simpler by just telling the client you're going to give a few minute's silence for them to go as deep as they wish, but I feel the numbers keep the conscious mind occupied whilst the unconscious mind does the deepening.

Finally, silence can be a good tool if you are using confusional techniques with a client. Pausing at unexpected places in a sentence creates a sense of anticipation as the client tries to guess what might come next, or of trust as they start to pause with you and simply wait and see.

There are plenty of ways in which you can use silence, and these are just a few. The main thing is not to think of silence as an absence but as a real and active part of your communication skills, so you can use it to your – and your client's – best advantage.

The role of therapist self-disclosure

I was once told that one of the most common client complaints about therapists was that the therapist never go to the client's problems because they were too busy talking about themselves. And a recent online discussion, about a client who asked a therapist what their political affiliation was before signing up for sessions, got me thinking about this topic. When does self-disclosure aid rapport and when is it intrusive?

Let's start by saying what we mean by self-disclosure.

Technically, multiple forms of self-disclosure go on in therapeutic settings – client to therapist, therapist to supervisor, trainer to student and vice versa for all of them. Professional self-disclosure from you to your clients, such as what qualifications and experience you have will, of course, need to happen regularly.

At the moment, we are focusing on what, if anything, you as a therapist should tell your clients about your personal life.

Of course, certain things about you can be observed and are therefore shared unavoidably; your race, gender, accent, etc. If you tell the client you will not be able to see them next week because you are on holiday, this is also a form of self-disclosure; especially if you answer questions about where you are going, who is going with you etc. Other facts may be shared more indirectly, such as wearing a religious symbol on a necklace, publishing a family photo on Facebook and forgetting to mark it friends and family only, or via your hobbies (if, for example, you bump into the client whilst attending a match at your local football ground).

Although, generally, we get to know another person by sharing personal details about ourselves equally in both directions, in therapy the information flow tends to be more of a one-way street, from client to therapist. So, when might it be right, or helpful, to share personal details about yourself with a client?

I should say up front that although I train hypnotherapists, I couldn't find any studies done on therapist self-disclosure in hypnotherapy, nor many scholarly articles.

The available studies seem to be based on counselling. But it seems reasonable to say that the communication between a hypnotherapist and their client is taking place in a similar context, so the findings of what I did discover should, logically, be broadly transferable.

Is therapist self-disclosure a good thing?

Unfortunately, this isn't a simple yes/no question. The shortest answer is probably 'It depends' – on you, your client, the kind of self-disclosure and the kind of issue you are dealing with. It may also depend on your theoretical orientation and the theoretical background your therapy has – some specifically require therapists to be a blank slate and give away nothing of themselves, while others encourage a more interactive relationship with clients.

Pinto-Coelho (2018) for example, says: "In successful Therapist Self-Disclosures (TSDs), the typical content was accurate, relevant similarities between therapist and client; typical consequences were positive. In unsuccessful TSDs, the typical antecedent was counter-transference reactions; the typical intention was to provide support; typical content involved therapists mistakenly perceiving similarities with clients, and the general consequences were negative."

In other words, the right bit of self-disclosure at the right time, where real similarities in context exist, can be helpful.

But if the client does not perceive the similarities, or if transference gets in the way, self-disclosure is unhelpful.

So, as Spinelli (2002) said: "the issue is probably not about whether or not a therapist should self-disclose but when should a therapist self-disclose?"

When therapist self-disclosure is helpful:

- Where the disclosure concerns elements of your professional experience such as qualifications, training, and experience
- Where genuine similarities exist and can be used to illustrate a point about the client
- To enhance the therapeutic relationship by offering a personal response, thought or feeling, often called the 'use of self', and most prevalent in humanistic counselling
- Where similarity is important to the client, for example, someone looking for drug or alcohol counselling may seek out a counsellor who has previously had issues with the same addictions
- Where you are reflecting a feeling or response of your own back to the client that is relevant to the therapy, for example, "I feel that you are not engaging with me as well as you usually do. Is that a perception you share?" Or, "I admire how hard you worked on that."
- When it validates the client's feelings as 'normal'.

When therapist self-disclosure is unhelpful:

- When it takes the focus of the session away from the client and onto the therapist
- Where it is done to fill some need of yours and not of your client
- When clients have boundary issues or ask questions

about your personal life that you don't feel comfortable answering

- Where it blurs professional boundaries. Studies have shown, for example, that sexual boundary violations between therapists and clients often begin with therapist self-disclosures that ignore the differences between a professional and personal relationship
- Where you are imposing your solutions on clients instead of helping them to find their own.

How should you self-disclose?

Carefully! Jokes, aside, always think twice before offering a self-disclosure.

It can be tempting, especially if you are inexperienced, to let a session turn into a general chat. If the only people you see all day are your clients, you might feel isolated or miss the camaraderie and water-cooler chats you had in your previous job. However, it's not the role of your clients to fill that gap. That's where a decent support system of friends, family, supervision, peer support groups and even Facebook groups for therapists can come in handy.

The amount of self-disclosure you are comfortable with will vary depending on your personality, your theoretical approach and the type of therapy you offer to clients. It will probably vary between clients as well, although if you're noticeably more comfortable disclosing to some clients than to others, it may reflect your needs and preferences more than theirs.

Richard Schwartz, an American psychologist, suggests using the acronym WAIT before offering a self-disclosure. This stands for "Why Am I Telling?" and is designed to make you stop and think before jumping in there with personal details. So, before deliberately disclosing anything about yourself (other than professional details):

- Consider if projection or transference are involved – are the similarities between you and your client actually as strong as they feel to you?
- Consider whose benefit the disclosure is for
- Consider if the same information would be just as helpful if presented in a slightly different way, for example, in the form of a therapeutic metaphor, or as if it happened to someone other than you
- Consider how it might affect the client's view of you, and your professional relationship.

In the end, as with many things, you have to find the balance that's right for you.

The effective use of aversion

Some hypnotherapists routinely use mildly aversive techniques such as 'fork in the road', where the client is asked to compare the consequences of continuing an old behaviour pattern and taking a change of direction, or stronger ones like imagining their own death from smoking-related illness (sometimes with sound effects and even hospital smells added to create a more vivid experience). Others use aversion techniques occasionally, or even never.

It does seem unethical to deliberately upset your clients or scare them witless unless there's proof to show it's likely to be helping them, so I went looking for this evidence. I found very little, but what I did find might surprise you.

What is aversion therapy?

Behavioural psychology tells us that if we do something and the consequences are pleasant, we'll more than likely want to do it again. If we do something and the consequences are unpleasant, we'll probably try to avoid a repeat.

Of course, there is much more to behaviourism than that and if you want more detailed information you can check out Appendix Two at the back of this book.

That's broadly how aversion therapy works; it associates an unwanted behaviour (like smoking) with unpleasant feelings, ideas or experiences so that we no longer want to do it. We're going to stick with the example of quitting smoking as we move on, by the way. Although it is possible to use aversion therapy with many issues, most of the studies have been done on smoking and it's where aversion seems to be most often used. So, let's start with an example of how aversion therapy might apply.

The Mayo Clinic says that when someone smokes a

cigarette, nicotine entering the body triggers the release of dopamine, a neurotransmitter (brain chemical) that makes them feel good. Smokers also tend to associate smoking with specific activities: relaxing, socialising, 'me time' and so on, which associate it even more strongly with pleasant feelings.

These positive associations with smoking tend to make it hard to quit.

The behavioural theory says that we can help to overcome these positive associations by giving the client negative ones that are even stronger.

Look at it this way. Suppose you enjoy swimming and it has lots of positive associations – fun with your kids, wonderful holidays in the sun and so on. How much willpower does it take to avoid jumping into a pool full of man-eating (or woman-eating) sharks? The answer is none, because you know what will happen next. The sharks trigger negative associations that quickly overcome any enjoyment you believe you would get from the swimming.

If someone wanted to deliberately put you off swimming, putting sharks in your pool would be an aversion technique.

Does aversion therapy work?

In our swimming example, probably. Or at least you'd find another pool. But therapy is a bit more complicated.

Firstly, I have to admit that I couldn't find any studies comparing hypnotherapy that included aversion techniques with hypnotherapy that didn't. That's an idea for someone who fancies doing some research, I suppose.

However, there are some studies on aversion used with smokers in other therapeutic modalities. Generally, these involve either very rapid smoking of a large number of cigarettes, intended to make the client feel unwell, or pairing smoking with mild electric shocks, nausea or both.

Hajek and Stead (2011) searched the Cochrane Tobacco Addiction Group specialised register for studies that looked at aversive smoking cessation methodologies. Unfortunately for us, they decided that there was a, "relative absence of small studies with negative results . . . most trials had a number of serious methodological problems likely to lead to spurious positive results". In other words, most of the experiments were biased or too badly designed to be reliable. However, outside of that particular resource, there are a few studies that show more hopeful results.

According to Nigel Barber in *Psychology Today*, (2010) after undergoing the Shick-Shadel aversion therapy (pairing smoking with a combination of electric shocks and nausea), '52.5% of 327 people were still off tobacco after a year' although Barber notes, "Other studies of aversion therapy produced more modest results."

A meta-analysis study published in *The American Journal of Medicine* in June 2012 reported that, when compared to smokers attempting to quit without any therapeutic or chemical assistance, alternative quit-smoking treatments improved the success rate by factors of:

- Acupuncture 3.53
- Hypnotherapy 4.26
- Aversion therapy 4.55

The use of aversion techniques within a hypnotherapy session wasn't recorded but this does give some credibility to the idea that it can help our clients.

How much aversion does it take?

I've always felt – and told my students – that if you are going to use aversion-based hypnotherapy with smoking clients, you really have to go for it. Don't pussyfoot around but make it as strong as you can. This is based on my feeling that smokers must be pretty good at ignoring negative messages about smoking, since they are on every pack and most of the public health ads. I am gratified to say that I found some evidence to support this.

The 2011 Hajek and Stead report mentioned above cited an efficacy figure of 14% for rapid smoking and 7% for milder versions of aversion smoking. Although they had doubts about the reliability of some of the studies included, it does perhaps indicate a trend that stronger methods may have more effect.

Dinh-Williams *et al* (2015) compared MRI scans of smokers' brains when they were exposed to aversive images about smoking, aversive images about other issues and images likely to trigger a desire to smoke. They found that their brains reacted to the aversive smoking images much less than to the other two types, indicating a definite ability to ignore negative messages about smoking.

Where does this leave us?

Hajek and Stead seem to offer some support for my theory that you are better off using strong aversive stimuli than milder ones.

The Dinh-Williams study explains why this might be; smoking-related aversion has less impact on smokers than either other kinds of aversion or (most importantly for us) the triggers that encourage them to smoke. It makes sense that stronger forms of aversion are harder to ignore than milder ones.

As hypnotherapists we, therefore, need to consider our aversion approach carefully:

- The goal of aversion therapy is to create explicit negative associations with smoking, but they must be powerful enough to overcome the triggers that make the client want to smoke

- Smokers are good at ignoring negative messages about smoking, so strong aversion is probably more effective than milder forms
- Aversion needs to be combined with other, non-aversive ways of dissociating smoking from pleasure, which avoid the barriers that protect smokers from taking in negative information about smoking.

Of course, having got past any ethical issues and decided to use aversion, you have to ensure that you shock the client without leaving them completely traumatised. My approach to this is to use the aversion fairly early on in the session. Shock them into the decision to quit, then go on to build up happiness, determination, motivation and confidence with lots of positive suggestions, and end the session on a high.

So, am I recommending strong aversion therapy for every client?

I have to say, no. I don't think there is any technique which suits literally every client. Each quit smoking session should be unique to the client you are working with, including as many elements of their lives as possible – their hopes and dreams as well as their fears. But I now have some facts on which to base what was, before, only an intuitive decision and I hope I have given you some too.

Section 3 – Running Your Business

Practical paperwork and other admin matters

Insurance and tax

Risk assessments for you and clients

Reflective practice and how to do it well

The pros and cons of niching

Should you publish your prices?

Making the most of networking

How to get word of mouth referrals

Successful blogging

Practical paperwork and other admin matters

Paperwork is rarely people's favourite part of running a business, but it has to be done. (I might be an exception to that, as I quite like it. But then I came to therapy after years in the clerical civil service and my family say I think in paperwork!) Like it or loathe it, there are legal, ethical and practical reasons why keeping your records in order is a good idea and the key to keeping everything up-to-date and relevant is to make your system as simple and streamlined as possible. It's also worth mentioning that the advice in this article will apply whether we are talking about paper records or online/digital ones.

Records for you

Start by brainstorming a shortlist of forms, letters or documents you will need to take people from their first contact with you to the end of therapy *. The Therapy Loop chapter earlier in this book can help with this because it shows you how clients will move through your practice. Your list will depend on how you prefer to work, but it might be something like this:

- A first contact checklist (to be kept by the phone to ensure you get and give all the relevant information before booking someone in)
- Handouts, articles or leaflets to send to clients who ask for more information before booking. The best format is PDF since they are simple to email or download, and

* If you're recently qualified, you can do this even before you see your first client. If you're already in practice, and reading this section because you feel buried under an avalanche of admin chaos, you can take the same approach and then use the new system with all clients from a chosen date.

less easily overwritten than Word or Pages documents

- A diary, either paper or online, which is easily accessible at all times, so you can put client appointments in there as you make them, then you will never forget or double-book a client
- An appointment letter, confirming the place, time and date of your first appointment, prices and how to pay, cancellation policy, any actions you want them to take before attending (such as filling in your intake form, preparing a list of motivators etc.)
- Information to help clients find you, to be sent with the appointment letter. Include details of public transport as well as a map for those driving, and if they can't park on or next to your premises, make sure you give directions to a local car park
- An intake form to be completed by you in conversation with the client, or by the client before they attend for their first appointment; if this is online, ensure that the collection and storage of information on any third party system is GDPR compliant
- A GDPR compliant privacy policy - no need to reinvent the wheel with this one, you can get templates free of charge online or from some professional bodies, and simply insert your business details
- Terms and conditions or client contract to be signed at the first appointment
- A reflective practice pro-forma to use at the end of each session, or each set of sessions. (We'll look at this topic in more detail later in this section).

You could also consider having:

1. a confidentiality statement about how you use social media and/or testimonials if this is not already covered in your privacy policy

2. session notes pro-forma (again, I'll talk more about how to approach this particular task later in this section)
3. a follow-up questionnaire if you intend to use one
4. supervision and CPD records, ready to be filled in.

I like to use standard letters for the most important information such as appointment confirmations. These can be saved onto a word document or set up as 'signatures' on an email account so they are quick and easy to use, all you need to do is insert the client's contact details and the time and date of the appointment. It's a bit impersonal, true, but has many advantages:

- Everyone gets the same (correct) information
- You don't forget to include anything vital
- It saves time if you are having to send the same information to lots of people.

Unless you're using an automated version attached to an online booking system, you can always add the personal touch by adapting the first line or two to the particular client you're writing to. It might seem like overkill to have all this documentation prepared when you are still looking for your first client, or perhaps are only working with a couple of people, but as your business grows it will adapt and grow with you. Scribbling notes on the back of an envelope tends to be harder to upscale!

Records for other people

As a therapist you are collecting and storing sensitive information; not just names and addresses but also family, financial, medical and psychological information. This means that, once you have clients, you will need to register with the Information Commissioner's Office, which you can do via https://ico.org.uk.

You will also have to store client records appropriately;

broadly this means they must be password-protected if they are digital and locked up securely if not. As well as any tablets or PCs, you need to password protect any mobile phones on which you accept client calls, since callers' numbers will be stored.

Why you should keep good records

Keeping good client records has a lot of advantages to you as a therapist. They mean:

- If the client ever comes back to you for the same – or another – problem you can see at a glance which approaches suited them best
- If there is ever a query about what happened in a session, or a complaint against you, you can refer to your notes
- If a client ever asks for a copy of their notes, they will be able to follow and understand them. This is a requirement under the GDPR.

The same point applies if a client asks you to share your records with someone else, for example, another healthcare professional or their legal representative.

You should never provide copies of your client records to anyone without the client's permission in writing, unless required to do so by a Court Order or warrant, those last two are relatively rare but clients do sometimes ask you to share records with other people, using the GDPR right of portability.

I had one client, for example, who was seeing me for anger management after she lost her temper, lashed out and hurt someone else. Her barrister suggested she should obtain a copy of my notes to prove in court, should it become necessary, that she had acted on her own responsibility immediately after the incident to try to prevent such a thing happening again. Another client was suing his employer for work-related stress and wanted a copy of my records sent to his lawyer to prove the effect the stress had had upon him.

If this does happen to you, remember that the records you provide will be shared with the prosecution and the judge as well as the defence, so they need to be clear and impartial, offering a balance between recording your work with the client and respecting their privacy.

The Complementary and Natural Healthcare Council (CNHC), the UK Voluntary Regulator for complementary healthcare practitioners, recommends that your client records should be, "legible, attributable and truly represent your interaction with the client". Attributable means it should clearly show who has written what on the client's record, not much of a problem if you work alone, but it should be borne in mind if you share clients with other therapists.

Client records should be kept safely and in good condition for at least seven years according to most professional bodies and insurers, and eight years according to the CNHC*. If your client is a minor, you will need to keep them until that long after their eighteenth birthday. Something that few therapists seem to think of is that if you should close your practice or pass away during this time, the rules still apply; you should have arrangements in place for someone to take over this responsibility on your behalf.

* Complementary and Natural Healthcare Council. 2014. Code of Conduct, Ethics, and Performance, as updated 1 June 2018, paragraph B7. [ONLINE] Available at: https://www.cnhc.org.uk/sites/default/files/Downloads/CodeofConductEthicsandPerformance.pdf. [Accessed 8 April 2020]

Your client record won't just contain session notes, of course. It will also include: your intake form and the client's case history; a copy of their signed contract; any checks you did as to contraindications; your assessments of their needs and any formal assessments you used (such as GAD7); your therapy plan and any amendments that were made to it; the reasons that these changes were made; a note of any communications you had about the client with any third parties (e.g. your hypnotherapy supervisor); copies of emails/texts/correspondence or notes of any other contact with the client, for example, by phone; reflective practice pro-formas relating to this client. In short, any documentation relating to your work with them.

It may surprise you to know that, although session notes may well be the largest part of your client record, there isn't a standardised way of writing them up that is used throughout the hypnotherapy profession. There are guidelines available for formatting session notes if you choose to use them, but they are, I think, more familiar to counsellors than hypnotherapists.

There are several different versions of these formatting guidelines, but the one I have chosen to look at here is called SOAP. This is, of course, an acronym, meaning that each letter stands as a reminder for something you need to cover. Briefly, these are:

- Subjective – subjective information is about perception: how someone experiences and reacts to things, based on feelings or opinions rather than facts. The subjective part of your notes is often the longest, it includes much of the case history, along with how the client has been feeling since your last meeting, how well they feel they are progressing. For example, the client may say they are feeling generally more positive which is a subjective evaluation of how things have been going

- Objective – objective information is based on facts. It's measurable and observable and does not take account of feelings or opinions. This section will include any factual information the client gives you, or your personal observations. For example, you might record examples of language or actions that demonstrate their new positivity, or the amount by which they have reduced their weight
- Assessment comes next – this is your professional opinion about how well the client is doing, comparing their progress with your therapy plan and their goals, to check whether things are going in the right direction
- Planning is the final stage – a look ahead including any actions to be taken by either you or the client to move things forward. I'd include a note about what techniques or scripts you have used in this part.

Here's an example of SOAP notes based on a fictitious client who is undertaking hypnotherapy to help her reduce weight. Her initial goals were to eat smaller portions of healthy food and to exercise more.

S – Lily reports that she is finding it easier to stick to her eating plan and make healthy choices about exercise. She feels proud of herself for the progress she's made and says she is starting to like what she sees in the mirror. There was a setback on Thursday when her husband tried to persuade her to share a bar of chocolate with him. She got very upset and he didn't seem to understand why. She felt he had broken his promise to be supportive and wonders if he understands how important it is to her to reach a healthy weight.

O – Lily went out for a meal with friends on Friday night and chose to eat salad and fruit, when they all had heavy meals.

She reports having dropped 14 lbs and gone down two dress sizes. She has a new hairstyle and increased confidence is indicated by her making more eye contact than previously. When talking about her husband her body language changed, she slumped in the chair and appeared tearful.
A – Lily is progressing well for both weight loss goals; she has both reduced her portions and undertaken regular exercise. Even though upset by her husband's actions she didn't eat the chocolate. She is now half-way to her target weight.
P – We'll continue with the original therapy plan, but agreed on an additional target of being more resilient when tempted to break her diet by others, especially her husband.

Hypnotherapy in this session:
Elman induction, peaceful place, control room metaphor to reinforce changes, protective bubble and anchor/trigger for resilience.

Before the next session:
Lily will continue to listen to my weight control audio daily. I will email her the URL of my blog containing resilience tips.

Pro-forma record
It would be easy enough to have a pro-forma in your records which recorded each session in the same way and using this type of format helps to keep your sessions focused and on track. This is especially useful with clients who tend to over-run, something we'll talk about again in the troubleshooting section of this book.

Insurance and tax

No matter what your business model, insurance is a must and you may need to be covered in a few different areas. The most essential of these are:

- Professional indemnity insurance (or malpractice cover) covers any claim made against you because of something you did as part of practising your therapy. For example, a client develops emotional problems which they claim were a result of your poor therapy skills
- Public liability insurance covers an event that is not a result of you practising your therapy, but which happened because (or while) you were doing so. For example, a client trips over a rug in your clinic and breaks a leg. If you are working from home, your home insurance policy may have a public liability clause, but it's unlikely to cover you for claims from paying clients.

You might also want to consider:

- Product liability (to cover audios, courses etc) if you are selling these in addition to offering therapy
- Business asset insurance or portable equipment cover (e.g. to cover your work mobile phone or laptop if they are lost or stolen)
- Office content insurance for equipment, furniture, buildings etc
- Copyright infringement cover – this will only cover you in certain circumstances, for example, if your infringement was accidental
- Employers' liability may be useful if you lend your therapy room to others; even if you don't have a contract of employment you may have some of the same liabilities as an employer, especially if they borrow your equipment

- Cyber and Data coverage, in case client records are ever hacked or stolen
- Personal accident – to protect your income if you can't work.

I would also enquire what will happen to your cover when the policy ends. According to posts on social media, several therapists who tried to suspend or cancel their policies during the COVID-19 lockdown were told that, if they did so, they would no longer be covered for work done before the cancellation, even though the policy was in force at the time. It seems that whether work done during the lifetime of a policy is still covered after it ends is dependent on the specific wording in the policy document and you need to know what will happen if you change providers or retire.

That's a long list, and you might not need them all. Luckily, all the elements you do need will tend to come within one policy on a kind of pick-and-mix arrangement, just check you have everything you need before you part with any payment.

If you are already insured to provide other therapies, adding hypnotherapy to your existing policy may be the most cost-effective option. I would shop around for the policy that suits you best, which may be the one with the most comprehensive cover rather than the cheapest.

Tax and National insurance

If you are working as a sole trader, you will need to register as self-employed with the tax and National Insurance offices. For this purpose, your first day of self-employment (trading) is the first day a client pays you, rather than the day you start trying to attract clients. The costs you incur in getting to that point are known as pre-trading expenses and most things that could have been claimed after you started trading can be claimed as pre-trading expenses. https://gov.uk or your accountant (if you have one) will tell you all you need to know.

You will need to keep accurate accounts showing your business's income and expenditure. Since many therapists seem to be portfolio workers, especially when first setting up, (i.e. they have other jobs as well) your tax allowance may have to be spread across more than one employment; making sure your financial records are up to date at all times will help you avoid being overcharged.

A scheme called Make Tax Digital is being phased in for the self-employed, which requires you to keep your accounts digitally and to have them linked to your tax office account. Although at the time of writing (2020), this currently applies only to companies and sole traders with a turnover (income before expenses) higher than the VAT threshold, the idea is to gradually roll it out to include everyone, so my advice is to use digital accounts software straight away. That way you get used to them and don't need to scramble to change your ways of working when the rules start to apply to you. Since this is a changing situation, anything I write here will soon be out of date, but you can search online for "Make Tax Digital" to find the latest information.

If you want to operate as a limited company, you will need to register with Companies House and follow their guidelines. There are a number of financial and administrative returns to be made by specific deadlines and you will almost certainly need an accountant to help you unless you have experience in this area. There are pros and cons to the different ways of setting up your business. Sole traders are affected by fewer regulations and can keep simpler accounts, but you are personally responsible for any debts your business incurs.

Risk assessments for you and your clients

Any business with five or more employees must, by law, have a written risk assessment, but most therapy businesses are smaller. You might well be the only person your business employs. Having said that, even though it's not a legal requirement it can be a good idea to have a written risk assessment as part of your ethical and best practice approach to running your business.

What is a risk assessment?

A risk assessment is just what it says. It's a brainstorming exercise to identify anything in your business that might cause you – or your clients – harm, combined with a plan to remove that risk, or at least reduce it as much as possible. A risk assessment looks at five main areas:

- Identifying potential hazards
- Identifying who might be at risk of harm
- Evaluating the level of risk and creating a plan to reduce or remove it
- Writing all this down and putting your plan in place
- Reviewing all this regularly.

What to put in a risk assessment

The potential hazards that exist in your workplace will vary, depending on where you work and the type of client you work with. Here are a few questions to help you identify some of them, but I'm sure you can think of others.

Risks to clients:

- Could the client be contraindicated for your therapy?
- Is the client classed as vulnerable and if so, what steps do you need to take to safeguard them?
- Do you need to alter your usual way of working for this

client? (For example, might a client on the autistic spectrum find the usual lighting too bright or the background music too loud?)

- Does the client have psychological or physical health problems that might impact on the therapy in some way? (For example, is your usual chair comfortable, if they have a bad back?)
- What would you do if the client identified a duty of care issue such as child endangerment, self-harm or suicidal thoughts?
- Are there loose wires, or other trip hazards in the area where you work?

You may already ask some of these questions in your intake, without necessarily using the term 'risk assessment' to describe it. But thinking about it in these terms can be helpful to ensure you are keeping your clients safe.

Risks for you

If you work at home:

- Do you publish your full address online? (Not a great idea, the road name, area, or just the postcode should be enough to help clients decide if they can reach you. Give out the full address only when they have booked an appointment.)
- Do you ask clients to bring something to verify their identity?
- Are photos of children or family, or valuables displayed in your therapy room? (My householder insurers used to worry that clients were only there to 'case the joint'. The first year I saw clients at home I remember a note on my policy that if a burglary turned out to have been committed by a client, I wasn't covered. They're more understanding now.)

- Do your clients have access to any areas of your home that are not connected with your business? Do you accompany them as they move around your home, for example, on the way to the toilet?

Working online:

- How secure is the online platform you are using? Is it GDPR compliant?
- Will you be overheard, or interrupted? Will the client?
- What would happen if the connection was broken mid-session?
- Is it clear to the client which country's laws and regulations you operate under if they are not in the UK?

Working from clients' homes:

- Does someone know where you are at all times? This, of course, has to be balanced with the need for confidentiality but a record of your movements could be left somewhere secure, to be accessed only in an emergency
- Can you have a buddy system? Phone someone as you arrive and leave each address to let them know you are safe, you don't need to mention where you are or who you are seeing, simply that you have arrived at or left your 10 am appointment, for example
- Can you arrange an initial meeting with the client away from their home to ensure you feel safe with them?
- What do you know about the client before you turn up on their doorstep? What do you know about other people who may be in the building?
- Will your car be left in a safe, well-lit area?
- Do you carry a torch if you are making home visits in the evenings?
- What would you do if you felt unsafe? Could you carry a personal safety device or install an app on your phone?

Wherever you work:

- Do you screen clients before a first session, or can anyone use an automated booking system and attend without contacting you?
- Do you assess the risk to you from each client, and how likely they are to cause you harm?
- How could you exit the room quickly if a client's behaviour made you feel unsafe?
- If there is only one exit, who sits nearest to it – you or your client? (It should be you.)
- Do you have an emergency contact in case the client is taken ill?
- Are you at risk of allegations about unethical behaviour?
- Do you have adequate supervision and self-care arrangements to help you deal with upsetting or distressing experiences?
- Do you have firm client boundaries, for example making it clear how (and how often) you can be contacted between sessions?

Practical and environmental risks

- Do you have adequate and appropriate insurance in place?
- Is all flooring free from tears, holes and any trip/slip hazards?
- Is all electrical equipment PAT tested regularly to ensure it's safe?
- Could some clients have difficulties in accessing your therapy room or the toilets (e.g. because of stairs)?
- Could anything in your work environment trigger allergies, for example, aromatherapy oils or air fresheners? What about if you work from home and have a cat or dog?

Create a chart like this:

1. Column one – the hazards you think might exist in your practice (one risk per line).
2. Column two – who is at risk of harm in each case.
3. Column three – the nature of the risk.
4. Column four – how high the risk is and why.
5. Column five – what can you do to remove or reduce the risk of that harm?
6. Column six – the date you have taken this action.

An excel spreadsheet is fine for this, but you can download free risk assessment forms from a variety of places online such as https://www.myriskassessment.co.uk

Now you have a risk assessment . . .

All you have to do is put your action points in place and make sure you review it from time to time. This last point is essential because things change, for example, a carpet which is fine now, might develop a tear in a few months and create a new opportunity for someone to trip and get hurt.

Reflective practice and how to do it well

It's a bit of a cliché that therapists learn from every client and here's another to go with it. We say we 'practise' rather than 'perform' therapy because we can always – no matter how experienced we are – get better.

But we can't just see clients, keep our fingers crossed and hope that learning happens. We need a way to ensure that it does and reflective practice is one way to achieve that. Unfortunately, reflective practice doesn't just happen either, and we need an effective way to go about it.

Why should therapists carry out reflective practice?

- To increase self-awareness of how and why we make our professional decisions, so that we can make them more effective instead of falling back on habit
- To undertake critical evaluations of the ways we are working, so we can improve our skills and get better results for our clients
- To develop creative thinking skills to help us focus on the client in front of us
- To aid the process of supervision, and decide which clients need to be discussed with a supervisor
- To identify areas where our practice could be improved, perhaps by CPD
- To identify which skills and approaches work best, so they can be utilised most effectively
- To support self-care, by offering understanding as to how we felt about working with a particular client as well as what we did and how it worked.

Carrying out reflective practice means that we look critically at our professional activities to understand why we made the decisions and choices that we did in working with clients, so we can get better at making those decisions in the future. Levy (2020) called reflective practice the, "engine of life-long learning". You can undertake that learning yourself, or it may be something you do with a supervisor.

How often should you use reflective practice?

It's up to you. Some people find it best to reflect on each therapy session they do. Others carry out reflective practice after a specific number of sessions with a client, or at the end of working with each client. This last can be OK if you work with clients for relatively short periods. But if you are struggling to help a client, or maybe reacting emotionally to their issue, or working with them for a longer-term, I'd suggest carrying out reflective practice at regular intervals throughout their care. If you don't carry out reflective practice with all clients I recommend at least doing so with a random selection. Avoid focusing only on the ones that go well (or don't) or on those presenting with a specific issue.

How do I carry out reflective practice?

Dave Mearns (1997) designed a list of questions for therapists to ask themselves about clients as part of their reflective practice such as:

- How do I behave in relation to this client?
- What do I feel in relation to this client? (note, not about the client as a person, but 'in relation to' working with them)
- What do I think when I work with this client?
- What goes on underneath for me?
- What parts (aspects) of myself am I using with this client?
- Am I changing in relation to this client?
- What parts (aspects) of myself am I not using in relation to this client?

- What is the nature of my empathy with this client?
- Are there blocks to developing empathy with this client?
- How is my warmth with this client?
- Is my warmth different with this client than with others?
- Do I have a tendency towards conditionality with this client? (i.e. do I impose conditions such as completing add-on tasks at home which then influence my positive regard or empathy?)
- Am I feeling any problems in relation to my contract with this client?
- Do I have boundary problems with this client?
- What am I learning in relation to this client?
- What are my assumptions about how the client is experiencing me?
- How am I checking on the client's experiencing?
- What is my judgement (or assessment) of this client's locus of evaluation? (I.e.does the client assess information/situations internally (relying on their own judgement) or externally, based on what other people tell them they should think?)
- Is my judgement of the client's locus of evaluation affecting my communication with this client?

You'll notice that there is no assumption that you don't know what to do with the client or that you are struggling to get results. The same questions can be used with any client and may help you work out what goes well in your therapy as well as what can be improved.

This is a long list. If you find it a bit daunting, the general principles can be reduced down to:

- Describe briefly what happened with this client, including what both of you did and felt throughout the therapy
- Think critically about how well things went for both you

and the client, how well you worked together and why you each made the choices and decisions you did

- Think analytically about the outcome – was it as expected? If not, why not? What could you have done differently to improve things? What have you learned from working with this client that you could use with other clients? Did working with this client identify a need for CPD?

The easiest way to carry out reflective practice is to have a pro-forma or diary to complete. Check Appendix Three, and Appendix One to find one.

Your reflective practice records, of course, are part of your client records and should be stored securely in accordance with current data protection rules.

Having said that, it can be very useful to keep a copy of your reflective practice forms together as well as with individual clients' notes, and to file them grouped by the client's presenting issue.

That way if, for example, you are struggling to help a client with a flying phobia, you can easily flick through your reflections on working with other clients with that issue to see what you learned from them, and perhaps jog your memory about the various approaches that have been useful for you in the past.

Having your reflective practice forms handy can also be very helpful in supervision sessions, rather than having to wade through a full set of client notes.

And remember that, although we have been focusing on client work in this article, reflective practice is not just for clients. If you reflect similarly on other activities as well, such as books you have read, training courses you have attended etc., you will find you can get more benefit from them and better value for money from your CPD training.

The pros and cons of niching

Niching is popular at the moment, and many business gurus will tell you it's the way to go to grow your business. As with anything, there are pros and cons, so I'm going to indulge in a bit of self-disclosure. Bear with me, it won't last long and it's all in a good cause.

My Mum recently needed to consult a solicitor. Nothing earth-shattering, just for basic advice on wills after a change in circumstances. A firm we found said they offered, "legal advice for the elderly"; clear advice, no jargon etc. Sounds good, right? The guy she saw was friendly and helpful, everything was fine.

As it happened, not long afterwards I also needed some wills advice. Now, I have to consider myself middle-aged but haven't yet got quite comfortable with that 'E' word, so I emailed the firm my Mum had used to ask what age group they covered. Imagine my amazement when I got an email back asking me to ring them for a chat about it.

Wary of such obvious evasion on so simple a point I emailed again, asking even more directly. At what age am I 'elderly' enough to access your services?

Again, nothing back except generalisations. Eventually, after a few tries, they admitted they had no age limit and would be happy to help.

Getting back to the point, the reason I mention all this is that it demonstrates very clearly the debate about whether specialising is a good thing or not. If you're a generalist, you are there for everyone, but you risk not being seen as an expert in anything. If you're a specialist, you may know exactly what you're doing in your niche, but you risk people thinking you don't deal with anything else. So, is niching a good idea or not?

The pros and cons of being a specialist

The following table makes your choices clearer.

	Pros	Cons
Generalist	A wider range of clients. Lots of variety in your working day, stretching yourself and your knowledge. Good for those who haven't had time to build up specialisms. The challenges promote adaptability and 'thinking on your feet'. More opportunity to develop related 'filler' services (courses, ebooks, products etc) for quiet times.	You may feel obliged to work with issues that don't interest you. You risk being seen as 'jack of all trades and master of none'. You may have to refer on more complex cases. It's more difficult to advertise via a USP (unique selling point) and stand out from the competition. Too many competing demands can impact on your welfare or confidence.
Specialist	Increased respect from other professionals and clients. You can justify not working with issues that don't interest you. The opportunity to charge higher session fees, and work 'smarter not harder'. Your work is more often in-depth and challenging. You have a more streamlined work process. You benefit from increased job satisfaction /confidence in knowing an area so thoroughly.	Your niche advertising may 'put off' some clients with other issues, although some may still contact you to see if you also offer what they are looking for. You risk getting bored, or running on 'auto-pilot' and losing the creativity in your approach. You may come to feel there are limited CPD or supervision opportunities because you are already the expert (but don't get smug - I learn stuff from my students every day!). There may be increased competition if too many others have the same niche. Your practice can be slower to adapt if the market changes suddenly, and it can; think Coronavirus.

Of course, even as a generalist, you don't have to work with absolutely everything, and sometimes it's better not to if the client's issue touches on one of your own.

Here is an example. One of my graduates felt she didn't want to work with clients on smoking cessation because her impression was that many of them just want a quick fix. Her mother had died a slow and painful death as a result of smoking and she felt the emotional baggage from this affected the way she related to smoking cessation clients. Some years later, she does now accept these clients, but only if she feels they are completely committed to stopping smoking.

My personal feeling is that, unless you have expertise in another area already, when you first launch your practice you should probably aim to be a generalist. The major disadvantage to this is that it's harder to advertise to a specific group of clients, but you can get around this by running single issue advertising campaigns, just rotate different issues that you're prepared to work with.

Over time, you may find that there is a demand for a particular type of service in your area, or that you attract a particular kind of client, and this will help you choose a speciality that will work for you. One of my graduates discovered, for example, that despite having a generalist website and PR, she attracted large numbers of people with phobias and she had a ready-made specialism.

Once you've chosen your niche (or it has chosen you) you can use your CPD hours to develop your knowledge and skill base into a proper specialism.

How should therapists choose a specialism?

Well, as said above, sometimes your specialism chooses you. But if you want to go out and find one, here are a few ideas.

- Topic – specialising in working with a specific issue that interests you, such as childbirth or weight control
- Theoretical approach: specialising in, for example, analytical or CBT-based approaches
- Client group – specialising in working with children, older people, women or a specific group of people such as people from a Black, Asian or other minority ethnic background*
- Environments – specialising in school or work-related problems, for example.

If you do decide to specialise, you may find that over time your specialism changes. And that's fine. Your practice is entirely yours and you can take it in whatever directions you wish. Or you may thrive on the challenges of a broad-based practice and choose to stay as a generalist for the whole of your career. If it suits you and your clients, why not?

* But be careful not to contravene anti-discrimination laws if you specialise in working with a group defined by gender or race, for example. We'll discuss this in more detail in the Q&A section at the end of this book

Should you publish your prices?

Let's start with the obvious. Along with wanting to know if the therapy will work, price is one of the things that every therapy client asks. Many of them have not used a therapist before and have no clue whether your sessions are nearer £5 or £500.

A lot of businesses consider it essential to put their prices online, and when you're selling a product like shoes or tins of peas this seems very sensible.

Imagine buying from a site like Amazon or eBay if they removed their prices! But when you're selling a service, like therapy, it's not just about the price, it's about value, and you might feel that publishing prices doesn't allow you to demonstrate that value. So, how do we resolve the question about whether or not to put them out there for all to see?

Understanding cost, price and value

Let's start with some definitions. As a therapist, you are almost certainly a business owner as well, and it's worth getting your head around some business concepts. This is one of the most important, and understanding it can affect your decisions about both how you price your services and whether you publish those prices for all to see:

- Cost is how much you, as a business owner, have to pay to provide your services; your overheads. It includes not just the price of your therapy room, but also your travel expenses, the production of any materials you use (leaflets etc), and the wider expenses involved in keeping your business afloat: training, professional memberships, insurance, phone, advertising etc.
- Price is what the client has to pay, in monetary terms. Your fee in other words.

- Value is what your client gets out of seeing you. Not just, "I'm not afraid of flying any more," but what not being afraid of flying allows them to do. Whether they have better holidays, see family who live abroad, or fly for work, they get value (hopefully) for many years to come after the therapy sessions end
- Both cost and price are very practical, objective figures and can be calculated and expressed in terms of 'how much money?'
- Value isn't financial. It is the reason the client is prepared to invest time, money and effort into undertaking therapy.

These ideas can help if you feel you should charge less because, for example, you work from home and don't have many overheads, or have only recently qualified. Costs and prices vary, but the value of your service is just the same.

When you set your prices, you have to start with your costs, because there's no point operating your business at a loss. Unfortunately, there are always bills or price rises that you forgot to include in your calculations or didn't know about. If you are only charging a little over your basic costs these changes can quickly erode your profits and put you out of business. If your pricing is value-led, you can charge more without feeling guilty about it. And if this sounds a bit mercenary, remember that having a financially sound business and helping people are not mutually exclusive goals.

Now, let's go back to our original question – about publishing your prices – with all that in mind.

Unfortunately, publishing a figure on your website doesn't reflect anything but price. And although some clients will see the true value of what you are offering, others won't. This is pretty much the publish/don't publish argument.

Reasons not to publish your prices:

- It eliminates the possibility that the client sees the price and decides it's too expensive without considering value, sometimes called 'sticker shock'
- It encourages 'value conversations'; people who are already interested in what you offer will call or email, and you can help them see the full value they'll gain from seeing you before you give them the price
- Other local therapists (i.e. your competition) might see your prices and undercut you
- Your prices might vary depending on what the client needs, so a price list could be confusing (although you could publish a guide, perhaps with some anonymised case studies illustrating the top and bottom of your range).

Reasons you should publish your prices:

- You might prefer to let clients who are primarily price-oriented go elsewhere
- It reassures clients who might assume you are more expensive than you are
- It gives transparency and allows potential clients to make informed choices
- It reduces the amount of time you spend on the phone or answering emails, because those who might quibble about money, or who can't (or don't want to) afford you don't get in touch
- SEO (search engine optimisation) on your website – if someone searches online for, "price of hypnotherapy in my area" and you're the only one with a prices page, you will most likely come up high in the search results. If you're the only one who doesn't publish prices, your website may not come up at all.

How to decide

In the end, the choice is yours, but remember that looking at the price without considering value is making a decision based on incomplete information. On the other hand, depending on where you work and who with, many of your clients may have a limited income.

Just a personal aside here. I have never fully gone along with that idea that says: "If you make them want it enough, they'll find the money."

Yes, it works for some but, for most people, however well they understand the value of what you are offering, the price is likely to be a consideration. It really annoys me if I email someone to enquire about prices and get back a blurb about how wonderful their staff/services are, or an invitation to phone them, with no price included. But maybe that's just me.

Going back to your clients, you could try to make value clearer on your website. Maybe include a 'what else can you buy for this?' blog showing how your prices compare with a dinner out, a plumber's callout fee, a tank full of petrol etc. Or some client stories (with permission and suitably anonymised) demonstrating how working with you has impacted long-term on people's lives.

But, in the end, value conversations are often best held in person because they are so subjective that they will vary from one client to another.

In conclusion

There's nothing to stop you having your prices on the website at some times, and removing them at others. Experiment and see what works for you. However, here's my general guide.

You should publish your prices if:

- You have plenty of clients and would prefer to spend more time seeing them and less on answering casual enquiries
- You have a website which is crammed with information that makes the value of your service obvious
- Your services are well-defined and contained, for example, you have a set price per session or packages.

Don't publish your prices if:

- Your prices vary depending on circumstances
- You would like more clients and want to encourage people to call you
- You are a good salesperson and enjoy talking to people about the value of your services.
- You have a high conversion rate from calls and emails.

Making the most of networking

At the time of the Coronavirus pandemic, our thinking about networking had to change. Social media has its place in making us feel connected to the world, and there are some great groups out there, but for many of us, posted discussions are just not the same as holding a conversation, whether that's by phone, Skype/Zoom or face-to-face. But at this time many of us got more used to online communications and saw their value. Whether we network online or offline there are two main reasons to do it:

- Meeting other therapists to build up a network for support and referrals
- Meeting people in other lines of work to get contacts for business services we might need, and/or to introduce ourselves to potential clients.

So, given that networking is going to cost you time and quite probably money, how do you make the most of it?

Networking with other therapists

The Cambridge dictionary defines networking as: "the activity of meeting people who might be useful to know, especially in your job." (*CED* 2020).

As hypnotherapists, we often work on our own and don't get the benefit of being around colleagues as often as other people. It's not just talking about work or sharing work experiences we miss out on, it's the five minutes downtime here and there – what is sometimes called water cooler chatting. It's usually not appropriate to chat about our families or last night's television with clients, so we need to get that elsewhere.

A group of researchers at MIT measured the impact of workplace socialising and found that workers who felt connected to colleagues have greater job satisfaction and were around 10%-15% more productive. Fair enough, that was in an office where people were surrounded by others but it's not too much of a stretch to say that those who work alone or remotely would feel something along the same lines.

Networking with other therapists offers you this informal aspect of working with others. Plus, they understand the pressures and joys of the work you do, and can perhaps offer support and advice if you are struggling with elements of your business or client work (within the limits of confidentiality of course).

The best way to meet other therapists, other than those social media groups, is often at support group meetings. These may be simply social events or based around CPD or supervision. You can also get to know other therapists when attending CPD courses – always take some business cards to workshops and similar events, and make sure you hand them out to everyone.

It's a good idea to find out who else is working in your area, most hypnotherapists are friendly and supportive in my experience and you may be able to work together on some projects or PR instead of competing.

You can also build up a referral network, so if you are super-busy, on holiday, or not so well, you can point any clients who don't want to wait till you can see them, to someone reliable.

You can also pass on clients with issues you choose not to work with, or who find it impossible to attend during your appointment hours. I'm not suggesting you give away half your business here, of course. Referrals should be a reciprocal arrangement, so you'll receive clients from your network as well as refer them on.

Networking with those in other lines of work

Those in other lines of work may be potential clients themselves or know someone else who is. Or they may provide services such as accountancy or web design, which you want to purchase.

You can do this kind of networking anywhere – just mentioning what you do to friends or people you are chatting with when you walk the dog can help get the word out there. But there are also formal opportunities such as breakfast meetings, small business owners' organisations and various online groups.

Most of these groups frown on hard sell techniques, it's a more subtle approach of getting to know people and what they offer, so you can get in touch with one another when needed. As above, this should be a two-way arrangement; bear in mind what you can do to help other people's businesses as well as what they can do to help yours. Attending with a friend can be useful, you can talk positively about one another's services without appearing boastful or pushy.

If you are meeting in person, ensure you have business cards with you so you can leave people your details easily if it seems appropriate. Collect business cards as well as giving them out, and write a quick note on the back of each one about the person. Reading through these before attending the next meeting helps you remember who was who. If you are meeting online, make a list.

A couple of things to remember

Be prepared – always know before you go to a networking opportunity what your main purpose is, whether that's to build up a referral network or promote your business. It's hard to do both at once. Check the dress code if you are meeting face-to-face, most groups are quite laid back, but others are formal.

I can't say this enough, always carry business cards. Consider putting a QR code on them (like the one shown) so details can quickly be scanned into people's phones. You can get these created free online at sites like https://www.qrcode-monkey.com

How to get word of mouth referrals

Many successful therapists will tell you that they get a significant number of clients via word of mouth referrals, meaning that new clients are referred to them by previous ones. It's a great system since it means someone else is enthusiastically doing your marketing for you for free. Studies such as Khalid (2020) show that 88% of us put our faith in word of mouth recommendations from people we know. If you're not getting these clients, you need to take some affirmative action to ensure you do.

Why don't you already get word of mouth referrals?

- You assume that satisfied clients will automatically recommend you, even if they rarely do
- You feel uncomfortable asking for referrals, you're a therapist, not a high-pressure salesperson
- You don't want to look as if you're desperate for clients or to put clients under pressure to do you favours
- Your client has misunderstood the confidentiality rules and thinks they are not allowed to tell people they have seen you (rare in adults, but I have come across it)
- You worry there might be confidentiality issues around asking clients to tell people they have been to see you.

Regarding that last point, we must be absolutely respectful of confidentiality, of course. Similar worries lead some therapists to decide against using rating sites or publishing testimonials, both of which are popular word of mouth type promotions in most other fields.

However, there are plenty of things you can do to increase referrals without compromising your ethics or confidentiality, so, expand your comfort zone a bit and take action!

Why are word of mouth referrals worth having?

- 75% of people don't believe advertisements, but 92% believe brand recommendations from friends
- People are four times more likely to buy a product or service when referred by friends
- Word of mouth generates twice as many sales as paid ads. (Sukhraj 2018)

Of course, these days, word of mouth doesn't just mean chatting to people. It could also be a satisfied client posting about how you have helped them on social media or putting a review up on your Facebook page.

How to get word of mouth referrals

- Ask (tactfully and politely) all your satisfied customers to spread the word
- Ensure that you provide excellent customer service, so clients think you're worth referring to — not just the therapy but the whole package: a friendly and informative website and timely, efficient responses to telephone and email enquiries
- Answer questions openly and honestly. One of the highest number of referrals I ever had from one individual came from someone I never worked with. I was newly-qualified and felt I didn't have the right experience to work with him, so I referred him on to someone who did. He kept telling people: "If she can't help, she'll say so," and referred about a dozen people my way. I worked with all of them successfully
- Offering presentations about your services can help people become comfortable with you, I used to chat to Women's Institutes and similar groups. Overt advertising was frowned on, but they were quite happy for me to leave a supply of leaflets on the table.

Members often passed them on to members of their families and one client presented for therapy three years after the talk had been given

- Thank people who do make referrals: remember confidentiality and don't mention the name of your new client in your thank-you note, call or text, of course
- Consider some sort of referral scheme, via a specific programme (make five referrals and get a free relaxation session, for example) or something more informal
- Consider a reciprocal agreement with someone who provides a service that complements your own. If you're a hypnotherapist who works with weight-control clients, for example, you might recommend your clients to a personal trainer, who in turn refers their clients to you. If you work a lot with stress or anxiety, set up an arrangement with someone who does aromatherapy massage, and so on
- If you're a specialist, network with other therapists and let them know you are an expert. Offer advice and support, but also be clear (not pushy) that you will accept referrals if they have a client outside their area of expertise
- On social media, instead of a constant barrage of advertising, use the 'Three Es':
  1. Engage with your followers (post regularly, ideally at least two or three posts a week).
  2. Equip them with reasons to share your posts or talk about you (post engaging, useful and interesting things, not just a barrage of advertising).
  3. Empower them by asking them to share opinions of what you do and what they would like to see you do (ask questions and run surveys).

The best ways to request referrals

As I've said a few times in this section, you're not just a therapist, you're a business owner as well, and that means (among other things) promoting yourself. Asking for referrals in the right way doesn't make you look desperate or pushy, just professional.

If it's hard for you to ask, remind yourself that the worst that can happen is the client says, 'No'. If that happens, have a graceful reply ready which makes it clear you are quite happy to respect their preferences. Avoid arguing or making jokey remarks like, 'Oh well. Worth a try.'

Separate asking for referrals and taking money from the client.

Ask face to face, don't send an email or text after the client has left your office. It's more respectful and they're more likely to say yes.

Avoid putting pressure on clients by leaving them free to decide whether or not to act on your request. For example, at the end of every successful course of therapy give your client three business cards. One saying, "in case I can help you with anything else in the future," and the others to pass on to anyone the client knows who might benefit from working with you. This doesn't put pressure on the client, they could throw the cards away as soon as they get home if they want to. But it does let them know you are willing and able to accept referrals.

Successful blogging

Does the very idea of blogging make you throw up your hands in horror? You're not the only one, but read on, I may be able to help with that.

As small business owners, we are often told that blogging is good. But what is a blog? And why should we bother?

The term blog comes from 'web log'. They were originally a sort of online diary, with brief entries telling people what you (or your business) were getting up to today. These days, that sort of post seems to be used more on social media sites like Facebook, and blogs have become more like a library of articles. So, broadly, a blog is an article.

Why blog?

- Search engines tend to favour websites that are regularly updated. It helps them distinguish between sites that have been set up and abandoned, and those which are active and relevant, so they often list them higher in search results
- Adding a new blog regularly proves to them you are actively promoting your business
- It's a useful source of content for your social media pages, newsletters etc. If other people like or share your links it helps to spread the word about your business
- It demonstrates you know what you are talking about and helps connect you with other therapists who see these links; they can form a support or referral network
- It helps to connect you with potential clients. If you're offering free tips and advice, via your blog, they begin to build a relationship with you which might encourage them to pick up the phone for an appointment

You can test what your audience likes to hear about and

what they are interested in by monitoring which blogs get the most visitors, comments and interactions.

How much should you write?

Historically, as I've said above, blogs were short – often 200 to 250 words. Conventional online wisdom says that visitor attention span is brief and word length should be kept to a minimum, but Nick Schäferhoff (2018) argues that, the changed way that blogs are used means this probably doesn't apply any more. Have a look at these figures he's collected.

- Search engines tend to like longer pages, and the average number of words on a page that comes up on page one for a Google search is around 1900
- Articles over 1000 words get more shares on social media than shorter ones. (Not long posts, people can't be bothered to read them. But links to longer articles.)
- Human visitors to your website like posts that take about seven minutes to read (usually around 1600 words)
- The optimal word length for articles on healthcare topics is around 2000 words.

From all this, I'd say between 1000 and 2000 words seems to be a good target for therapists.

How often should you write?

Many sites on blogging tell you to post at least once a day. As a solo worker who has to do everything for your business from washing the floors to seeing the clients, this probably isn't possible. And it's obviously quicker and easier to fire off 200 words about your day than to write 2000 words on a topic you have to research. So how often you write may also depend on what (or how much) you're writing.

I'd advise you to write when you can but make it regular. Even if daily or weekly blogs are the gold standard, common sense implies that blogging once a month should be better than not doing it at all.

Set regular time aside every so often, maybe once a month, to write a blog and create social media posts. Schedule them to appear regularly. (Many social media sites let you do this. For those that don't, linking them to a free account such as hootsuite.com or friendsplus.me is invaluable, since you can schedule your posts from there.)

You can still add or share other posts if ideas or interesting tidbits of information come your way, but at least you know that a minimum number of items are going out, even when you're busy. If you can't commit to regular blogging, you might find places which accept guest blogs (one-off articles from someone other than the blog owner). That still gets your name out, and inbound links to your site, but without the regular commitment.* If you are listed on any directory sites, these often have a blog option, and this has the advantage that they usually promote your articles on their social media. I accept some guest blogs on my training blog, Hypnotherapy Training and Practitioner, so you could always drop me a line.

What should you write?

First, ask yourself a couple of questions:

- What's your passion? What do you like to talk or write about?
- Who is your audience? What are they interested in?

I'm broadly assuming in this article that you are writing for

* Read the T&Cs, though, to be sure who will hold copyright for anything you publish on someone else's site. If it's not you, you can't re-use the content.

clients, or potential clients, but if you work with corporate stress, for example, you might be aiming at employers. If you niche your therapy, you are writing for the people who need your niche skills.

Remember this. What your typical reader is interested in isn't therapy. (How many people do you think list 'hypnotherapy' as an interest on social media, for example, unless they are hypnotherapists?)

It may be wellness, weight loss, complementary therapy, health, or even yoga. So don't limit yourself to blogging only about what you do. Cover topics less directly related to what you do, as well as the specific areas you work in. So, if you work with people suffering from anxiety and stress, writing about improving happiness, positivity or satisfaction with life is likely to attract their attention.

This has the added benefit of allowing you to write about positive feelings, thoughts and habits, where your sales pages might focus more on the issues and problems faced by your clients. By all means, include a quick plug for your services at the end, but no-one will read a 2000-word advert!

'Listicles' (list-style articles) are very popular; titles like '7 tips to improve . . .' or '10 things to avoid when. . .' get people's attention and can be fun and easy to write. Mix these in with longer, more factually-based pieces to give your readers some variety, then keep an eye on which approach gets the most readers. Adapt your approach over time to produce more of the type of article which attracts the most likes, feedback or comments.

It's a really bad idea to copy other people's blogs. Not only is it a breach of the original author's copyright but Google penalises duplicate content on websites. However, looking at what others have said about your topic might give you ideas for an angle – how to approach it.

How to write

Everyone writes differently but here's my process to get you going.

Getting inspiration:

- If you use social media, you might get ideas about what to write from questions posted on groups you belong to, especially if a similar question is posted a few times by different people
- Think about what your clients most often ask you, in person or by email – answer that
- Have you been on a CPD course recently? Did that give you new tips you could pass on?
- What about the news? Has a celebrity recently admitted to having hypnotherapy for stage fright? Write an article giving tips for performance anxiety and refer back to the news article
- Is there a new study out about dieting, anxiety or quitting smoking that's been on the news? Talk about that and how it fits with what you do. (Tip: The YHT Facebook page often posts links to articles that you could use, and our monthly newsletter always includes at least one link to some relevant research.)
- Check out websites listing commemorative days, weeks and months for ideas. International Stress Awareness Month or Healthy Eating Week can inspire you and make your blog topical. (Be careful not to imply you are part of the official campaign, though, so as not to infringe anyone's copyright, and don't use official logos without permission.)

Putting together your content:

- Get something down on paper, (or more likely, a screen) focusing on ideas rather than detail
- Brainstorm, putting down even the sillier ideas. Notes,

words, phrases, slang, whatever comes to mind. Then start to organise it into some sort of logical progression

- Start to write, filling out each point, linking your ideas together and smoothing out grammar, structure etc. (And editing out the sillier elements, of course!)
- Spell and grammar check – twice! If this aspect of writing is not your forte, get someone else to read it as well
- I find reading the article aloud is a really good way of checking that the words, sentence length etc. work well
- I pick my title at the end, so it directly reflects what is in the article.

Images are important, to catch people's attention, but always ensure they are royalty-free or take them yourself. Some royalty-free sites have specific terms and conditions which apply to using their images around sensitive topics. Generally, this means graphic violence or sexual content, but anything about mental health is considered by some to be sensitive as well. I always include a disclaimer that the illustrations I use are stock images, posed by models, especially if there are recognisable people in them.

There might be other limits placed on your use as well, such as whether the images are OK to use commercially, and whether they are released for creative or editorial purposes, so check the T&Cs before using them and contact the site owner for advice if there is any doubt.

You're now ready for publication: press the publish button and go!

How to make the most of your blogging time

I've advised you to put regular time aside for blogging and scheduling social media posts but, as a busy entrepreneur, you need to make the most of that time. Once you have spent time and energy on producing a blog, it seems a shame to only use all that effort once. Recycling is all the rage and you can recycle information just as easily as anything else.

However enthusiastically you promote your blog, it's unlikely to be seen by everyone who follows you on social media, or by all your potential customers. Getting the same information out there in as many different ways as possible not only maximises the benefit from the time you've invested, but allows more people to see the information you have so painstakingly put together.

Your most popular blogs can be recycled or re-purposed.

Blog content can be tweaked to create ebooks, leaflets, or courses for your clients, or articles for publications. Even books. Listicles, in particular, can be converted into eye-catching social media image posts, with one bullet point on each image.

Run a themes of the month and schedule them to fall onto your page at regular intervals. If people have an interest in what you are talking about, and know you are talking about it regularly, they will make more effort to see and share your information.

Section 4 – Troubleshooting

Contraindications and medical referrals

Paradoxical (relaxation-induced) anxiety

Learned helplessness

What to do when therapy isn't going well

Clients who don't turn up

Problems with payments

'Difficult' clients

Contraindications and medical referrals*

I suspect I am opening a can of worms (hopefully metaphorical rather than medical) by covering this topic, but I thought it was worth looking at because there are so many conflicting bits of advice out there for hypnotherapists and not many answers.

What are contraindications for hypnotherapy? Is there a list somewhere? Do you need a doctor's permission to work with a client? And if so, when?

Each training school, and sometimes each therapist, have their own answers to these questions. If you try posting on social media, you'll get a plethora of advice, each response contradicting the last. I once saw a post which said we would be guilty of discrimination if we turned away those with serious mental health conditions, an assertion I completely disagree with by the way.

I can only give you my personal view, of course, but I'll work my way through the various bits of advice and legislation available and try to come to some conclusions.

Medical referrals

There is a variety of registering bodies for hypnotherapists in the UK and, although their Codes of Ethics cover broadly the same things, they word them differently. Some are more specific than others about when you need a medical referral. That's probably because Codes of Ethics have to cover all people in all situations and therefore need to remain focused on principles rather than specifics. I've chosen a

* It's important to say that I'm in the UK and the ideas I'm going to show you come from there. If you are practising elsewhere, I'm sure different rules will apply.

couple of examples as illustrations but, if you are developing a contraindications and referrals policy for your therapy business, you will have to begin with whatever Code of Ethics applies to you.

The General Hypnotherapy Register (GHR)

The GHR's Code of Ethics has two things to say specifically about medical referrals, which are:

- ensure that wherever a client is seeking assistance for the relief of physical symptoms, that unless already having done so, the client be advised to contact a registered medical practitioner. (Clause 8)
- never knowingly offer advice to a client which either conflicts with or is contrary to that given by the client's registered medical advisor/s. (Clause 9)

Firstly, you'll notice that Clause 8 only applies if the client is "seeking assistance for the relief of physical symptoms", so your first job is to decide what that means. Pain relief or menopausal side effects? I'd say yes, definitely. But what about anxiety? It often has physical manifestations. What about weight control? Is being overweight, in itself, a physical symptom?

I would tend to interpret this one on a case-by-case basis, using what I like to think of as common sense. So, for example, if a client with anxiety has distinct physical symptoms that could be caused by something else (if a client reported pain in the chest and down the left arm during panic attacks, for example, I would ask them to get it checked out immediately). If they are already being treated for anxiety by their doctor, especially if they are taking medication, I also advise them to let the doctor know they are working with me. That one is a bit of a stretch, perhaps, but seems like simple good manners.

It's worth knowing a bit about medications prescribed for issues like anxiety, you will have clients taking these. Not only does this help you check for contraindications, but if the physical symptoms mirror potential side effects, then referral back to the doctor is essential.

Now, going back to the guidelines, the second thing you'll notice is that they don't ask you to get a referral or permission from the GP, only to advise the client that their medical practitioner should be contacted. Nor do they say what form that contact should take, or what the client should say; it's left up to you decide what's appropriate for the client in front of you.

From this, simply asking the client to inform their GP they are seeing you should be fine. I recommend you either ask the client to sign something indicating they've been given this advice or record it in your session notes. Follow up at the next session: ask if they have done so and record their answer. If they have chosen not to follow your advice you will need to ask why and review whether you feel it's ethical to continue to work with them. If you're not sure, discuss the situation in supervision.

Most GPs, in my experience, when informed a patient is seeing a hypnotherapist shrug and say something fairly neutral and non-committal (although some are gratifyingly supportive). They're not being asked for an opinion, after all, just informed. But there is the possibility that the GP will say, "No. Under no circumstances. Don't do it!" or words to that effect. If that happens, you should stop working with the client (under clause nine), since to continue would be to contradict the advice given by the medical practitioner. This has only happened to me once in seventeen years of working with clients, so I'd guess it's pretty rare.

The Complementary and Natural Healthcare Council (CNHC)
In the UK, we are covered by a voluntary regulation system. Because it's voluntary, not everyone works or trains within it, but for those who do we can also look at the Training Standards, or Core Curriculum for Hypnotherapy. This is published by the Complementary and Natural Healthcare Council (CNHC), who describe themselves as: "the independent UK regulator for complementary healthcare practitioners". The training standards say how therapists should work and what trainers should teach if they are working within the voluntary regulation system.

The latest (2019) version* states that if there are possible contraindications therapists should: "contact the client's GP (always with the client's permission) or other relevant healthcare professional (such as a psychiatrist)." (para 9)

It says "possible contraindications" so, if you think the client might be contraindicated, you have to take action yourself and not simply advise the client to do so. If the client is definitely contraindicated, of course, you won't be working with them. Get the client's consent and then contact the relevant medical professional yourself. I'd say you will need this consent in writing, and it should include explicit instructions that information can pass both ways, between you and the GP and vice versa. Otherwise, you can contact them, but they can't respond because of GDPR and other confidentiality rules. A template letter to GPs is in Appendix Four, and is also one of the resources that can be downloaded from the our website. See Appendix One for

*Complementary and Natural Healthcare Council. 2017, amended 2019. Core Curriculum for Hypnotherapy. [ONLINE] Available at: https://www.cnhc.org.uk/sites/default/files/Downloads/Hypnotherapy-core-curriculum.pdf. [Accessed 5 April 2020].

how to access these.

The paragraph discussed above doesn't mention what it considers to be contraindications, of course, it just says how it wants you to deal with them. For what they might be, the best guide is paragraph 20, which says therapists should: "work within [their] competence, understand their limitations and refer on to another hypnotherapist or healthcare professional if appropriate."

So, working outside of your training is contraindicated, which seems quite reasonable. This doesn't prevent you from working with an issue for the first time, of course, but only in areas where you have knowledge or skills. This is still quite general though, and we have to look elsewhere for advice about specific contraindications.

There are some medical conditions widely (though not universally) considered to be contraindicated for hypnotherapy. The list you have, as we said earlier, will depend on who trained you in hypnotherapy and what issues you are trained to work with, but we can start to narrow things down a bit.

The Advertising Standards Authority (ASA)

According to its website, the Advertising Standards Authority (ASA) is: "the UK's independent regulator of advertising across all media". They apply the Advertising Codes, which are written by the Committees of Advertising Practice (CAP). Both ASA and CAP have a bit to say about what issues hypnotherapists can advertise they can work with. For example, CAP says: "Claims to offer treatment on conditions for which medical supervision should be sought are likely to be considered to discourage essential treatment unless that treatment is carried out under the supervision of a suitably qualified health professional (12.2)

"The ASA and CAP do not consider that hypnotherapists who do not hold a general medical qualification are likely to be suitably qualified to treat serious medical conditions.

"Claims to treat depression, addiction, eating disorders and other serious mental or psychological conditions are likely to be considered claims to treat serious medical conditions."

Just as an aside, the word addictions here doesn't seem to include working with smokers, as there are separate and specific rules about advertising to them. These can be found on the ASA website.

Back to the paragraph, and it seems they are worried that if someone sees you they will be less likely to seek out conventional medical advice. Whatever your view on that one, the rules apply anyway. Unless you have medical qualifications or other specific training in working with the relevant issue and a health professional overseeing your work, you should consider any serious mental or psychological conditions contraindicated. They give a few examples and, although it's not a comprehensive list, I've always considered that it would include psychoses like schizophrenia, or a severe personality disorder like psychopathy.

The next question is what do they mean by being supervised by a medical professional? It's possible that requesting a written referral from a doctor might tick this box, but I couldn't find any test cases to confirm that. If this situation comes up in your practice, I strongly recommend contacting CAP or your insurance and asking for advice before proceeding.

Overview

So where does this leave us? The ASA regulations are not

laws as such, because advertising is, like hypnotherapy, bound by a voluntary, self-regulatory code. However, they are designed to reflect the law and sanctions can be applied if the codes are broken. So, their rules apply to you and your practice whether you work inside or outside of the hypnotherapy voluntary regulations. And the GHR Code, although strictly speaking aimed only at their members, does seem to take a common-sense approach.

Unless you are covered by a Code of Ethics or similar that specifically requires another and different approach, here's my advice:

- Generally speaking, you don't need a doctor's referral to work with a client
- If you are confident you can work with a client safely and ethically, but they have physical symptoms as part of their presenting issue, advise them to contact their doctor. It's then up to them to do this
- There is no requirement to give this advice in writing, but it would be sensible to keep a record of some sort as proof you have done so, in case there are ever any queries
- This contact with the GP does not involve asking permission, but if the client's doctor advises against undertaking hypnotherapy, you should stop working with the client
- Never suggest or imply that clients should ignore a qualified medical practitioner's advice
- If you suspect the client might be contraindicated, it is your responsibility to obtain suitable permission from them and contact the doctor yourself
- You should only work within your training and competence. ASA and CAP say that they do not consider hypnotherapists qualified to work with: "depression,

addiction, eating disorders and other serious mental or psychological conditions" unless they hold medical qualifications and/or are supervised by a medical professional

Between them, these guidelines provide a kind of minimum standard, but you can always have stricter rules for your practice if you wish or adapt them to suit whichever body you are registered with.

I hope this will help you in your practice but please remember that this is written from my personal experience and is only intended as a guide. I am not an expert in the legalities of this area, and every client is different. So, if you are unsure how to proceed, err on the side of caution. Contact your insurer, supervisor, professional body, or CAP for advice.

This information is set out in a flow chart in the additional resources provided for readers of this book. Please see Appendix One to find out how to access them.

Paradoxical (relaxation-induced) anxiety (RIA)

As therapists – and perhaps especially as hypnotherapists – we tend to use relaxation techniques, breathing exercises and similar approaches to combat stress, but there are a few people for whom this can be counter-productive.

For them, techniques that are effective in reducing anxiety in most people seem to bring about an increase in heart rate and breathing, hypersensitivity and other symptoms generally associated with high levels of anxiety. This is called paradoxical or relaxation-induced anxiety (RIA).

Why does relaxation-induced anxiety happen?

Christina Luberto, a doctoral psychology student at the University of Cincinnati, has developed a Relaxation Sensitivity Index to help identify those who might experience RIA. (Luberto *et al* 2012). Luberto worked with 300 college students and concluded that about 15% of them were affected, although she estimates the figure is between 17% and 53% of those with chronic anxiety. She suggests that it could be due to:

- fear of relaxing generally
- fear of appearing lazy or unattractive in a relaxed pose
- fear of letting go or lack of control
- fear of the thoughts or memories that enter their minds when they are not constantly busy or distracted
- something in the relaxation triggering an old fear, for example, a colleague told me of a client who had once nearly drowned, and associated relaxation with going into that darkness. He had massive abreactions at first but felt better each time he practised
- fear of doing relaxation incorrectly
- dislike of the changes associated with relaxation, for

example, the switch from beta to alpha brain waves, or the dissociation that can come with meditating and self-hypnosis

- preference for high levels of activity and stimulation.

Michelle Newman and Hanjoo Kim at Penn State University, (2019) have a different take, they believe that relaxation creates an internal conflict in those who use worry as a coping strategy. In their view, worrying is a way of preparing ourselves for things that might go wrong, and relaxing interferes with that process. Unfortunately, as Newman points out, this can become a self-fulfilling prophecy. If we worry about something and it doesn't happen, we can become conditioned to continue worrying as a way of preventing negative occurrences.

Another theory is that it's down to something called contrast avoidance. In other words, people with anxiety may feel unable to cope with any changes in their emotional state, so it's more comfortable to stick with the worrying than to do anything to dispel it. Better the devil you know, as it were. Hanjoo Kim discovered that people with generalised anxiety disorders were the most sensitive to emotional shifts, while the effect was less noticeable in those with depression.

What does this mean for therapists?

Whatever kind of therapy you offer, from massage to the talking kind, if relaxation is an element, you could have clients affected by RIA.

There have been only a few trials of whether RIA has an impact on the use of relaxation training, and their conclusions aren't very clear. High levels of RIA seem to predict less successful outcomes to relaxation-based therapies on some measurements but not others. Studies by Newman, La Freniere and Jacobson (2016, 2018), for example, focused specifically on how patterns of RIA affected the outcome of therapy and found that although higher levels of RIA didn't necessarily predict poor outcomes, lower levels were associated with what they called "maximal benefit".

How can we help those with relaxation-induced anxiety?
It's important to say that RIA is not a medical condition or illness. It's not diagnosable as such and, in many people, it's not something that impacts their daily lives. They simply don't do much in the way of relaxation. Having said all that, it can be an issue in therapy if you want to help clients to relax as part of working with their presenting issue.

Every client is different, and their experience of RIA will be different too. Talk to them about their RIA: how do they experience it physically and mentally? What thoughts come into their minds when it occurs? Then work with what they give you. For example:

- If the client tends to worry more when they relax, use mindfulness to bring them to accept those thoughts and move on
- If the client worries specifically about being seen as lazy or unattractive when they relax, work on reframing this belief
- Stress that the client is in control throughout the therapy, and help to reduce the fear of letting go
- Provide a safe space for clients to explore shifts in emotion, and learn to cope with them
- Start your client with very short periods of relaxation (literally just a minute or two) and work up as they get used to the feelings associated with it
- Avoid relaxation-based inductions if you are working

with hypnotherapy and aim for only a light trance, especially at first

- Look for stress-busting activities that don't involve completely 'switching off', for example taking aerobic exercise.

Learned helplessness

Learned helplessness is something that happens when we are repeatedly exposed to an unpleasant experience that we are powerless to escape. It can be a big factor in preventing clients from moving forward, especially if they have lived with their problem for a long time, and/or tried and failed to deal with it in the past.

What causes learned helplessness?
Martin Seligman did many experiments on a phenomenon he called learned helplessness. (For example, Seligman 1972). In one, dogs were placed into a sling-like device and exposed to electric shocks. Group one could turn off the shocks by pressing a panel with their nose. Group two had no way to avoid the shocks, they simply had to be endured. A day later, the dogs were placed into a box where half the floor was electrified, and half wasn't. In this situation, they could escape the shock simply by jumping a low barrier between the two areas.

(Spielman *et al* 2014)

The dogs who had not been exposed to any shocks and those who had learned to turn them off all did this easily. However, six of the eight the dogs in the group who had been unable to escape the shocks in the first scenario never learned to jump the barrier in the second. They failed to recognise that the change of circumstances meant they now had a means of escaping the shocks. Seligman called this response learned helplessness.

Learned helplessness in therapy clients

It's thought that this learning pattern has parallels in human depression, stress, shyness, phobias, low self-esteem and motivational issues. Certainly, clients wanting help with behavioural changes like quitting smoking and reducing their weight will often say outright that they feel helpless, or make statements like, "I just can't seem to do it," as if their behaviour was out of their control, especially if they have repeatedly tried and failed to meet the same goal in the past. The effect of learned helplessness can kick in after only three failed attempts so I'm sure you can see how this might affect a client who has, for example, repeatedly failed to quit smoking. According to Seligman, learned helplessness leads to:

- Passivity when faced with trauma
- Difficulty learning that changed responses can control trauma
- Increased stress levels, with all the other elements that brings into the situation.

Not everyone who experiences trauma or failure will develop learned helplessness, of course. It's thought that this is to do with coping strategies, attitudes of pessimism or optimism and whether the client has an internal or external locus of control.

How to help clients experiencing learned helplessness

Underneath learned helplessness is conditioning – the client has learned (developed a belief or schema) that they are helpless to do anything about whatever their presenting issue might be. Our approach can be quite behavioural – recondition them to expect better – or quite analytical – find the source of the conditioning and undermine or reframe it. Here are some ideas:

- Offer unconditional regard, support and encouragement at each stage
- Metaphors – if you work with them – can be a really useful approach. Approaching learned helplessness directly can be very difficult for some clients. You could even use a story based on Seligman's dogs!
- Chunk the client's actual goal into much smaller steps that feel easier to take
- Work to improve self-esteem, especially using past situations where the client has been successful in creating change as a resource
- Identify repetitive negative thoughts or limiting beliefs and replace them with more helpful ones
- Increase optimism and positivity
- Undermine thoughts and behaviours that reinforce the learned helplessness
- Address the origins of the learned helplessness
- Build resilience to stress, anxiety and failure (we all fail sometimes)
- Help the client to identify elements of problem areas that they can control
- Encourage lifestyle changes and choices that reduce overall stress and anxiety levels
- Encourage the client to identify their own goals and solutions wherever possible

- Reassure the client that occasional relapses are normal, and that each time they are learning how to do better.

<u>*Understanding learned helplessness*</u>

When a person enters a new environment they assume a moderate level of control.
After an initial failure or setback, the person maximises their efforts to regain control
After three consecutive failures, the person starts to doubt that control is possible
After many failures, the person realises that the outcome is uncontrollable and personal control beliefs are replaced by beliefs indicating no control. *

**https://upload.wikimedia.org/wikipedia/commons/0/0f/Reactance_and_Learned_Helplessness_Model.png Sarah.Hugill [CC BY-SA (https://creativecommons.org/licenses/by-sa/4.0)]*

What to do when therapy isn't going well

There are many reasons clients may not progress as well as you had hoped. We're going to look at some of them here and also suggest a few things you can do to get things going again. Often lack of progress is summarily dismissed as due to secondary gain or resistance, or perhaps the belief that the client isn't ready to make the change. But is that really the problem?

Why might therapy not be helping your client?
I'm not saying that the reasons mentioned above are always wrong, but as ethical therapists, it is surely in our own best interests, and those of our clients, to look further. Other factors might be playing a part. Judith Pearson (2020) suggests we consider if the problem could be related to:

- Competing goals, the client can have result A or result B but not both
- Competing values, achieving the goal creates conflict between two equally significant values or beliefs
- Wanting the goal, but not having the strategies to accomplish it
- Wanting the goal, but not being prepared to put in the work required to achieve it
- Wanting the goal, but not the problems or responsibilities that might come with it
- Wanting the goal, but feeling blocked by limiting beliefs or fears rooted in past experiences

We could add to this:

- Is the client suffering from learned helplessness?
- Does the client have a personality (or personality disorder) that makes them deliberately manipulative or obstructive?

- Is there secondary gain in being 'incurable'? (Having seen multiple therapists of different kinds before you may indicate this is something worth exploring)
- Is the client only in therapy because someone else thinks they should be?

You'll notice that all these are about the client but, if we are honest, there are two people in this relationship and we need to consider our own input to the situation as well. This is where reflective practice and supervision comes in very handy. They will help you think about:

- Are you the right therapist to deal with this client?
- Could transference or counter transference be getting in the way?
- Are issues from your personal life interfering with your ability to offer therapy?
- Are there clear, measurable goals for the therapy, and a plan to reach them?
- Are you expecting too much of this client, or moving too fast?
- Are you failing to step outside your comfort zone when you need to?
- Is your rapport with the client good enough that they are telling you everything you need to know to help them?

Steps to avoid when therapy isn't working

It can be a difficult experience to work with a client who simply isn't progressing as you'd hoped. Especially if you are relatively newly-qualified, you can experience a kind of panic about what to do next. It's easy to fall for the idea that doing anything is better than doing nothing, but it really isn't. Your client has (perhaps) limited time and money to devote to therapy and will be aware that things are not going well. Consider your next move carefully instead of grasping at straws. Consider these points:

- Don't simply write the client off as 'hopeless' or 'not ready'. If they are still coming to see you, they want to change, and they still have faith in your help
- Review your approach by all means, but don't swing randomly from one thing to another, hoping to find something that makes an impact
- If you are inexperienced, think twice before asking for advice on social media groups. You'll get answers from people with many different backgrounds and points of view ranging from the practical to the esoteric, which may well be more confusing than helpful
- Don't take it personally if the client isn't completing tasks you give them to do at home or makes the same unhelpful decision repeatedly. Explore the reasons with them, look for ways to deal with the situation and read my notes on dealing with this situation, which you'll find later in this section
- Don't be openly or covertly critical in your questions or blame the client, stay neutral and empathetic
- Don't rush to force your ideas or solutions on the client. It may take longer for them to find their own solutions, but they will be more effective.

Steps to take when therapy isn't working

If we accept the NLP assertion that clients are not "broken" but using imperfect coping strategies as best they can, then we can still seek to give them better ones no matter what the reason for the lack of progress. So, what can you do to help get things moving again? Try to:

- Reassess your approach – using reflective practice and discussing things with your supervisor or a peer support group can be helpful here

- Discuss the situation openly and honestly with the client – do they share your perceptions that things are not progressing? Why do they think that is?
- Consider if their goals need refining, reviewing or chunking (breaking into smaller steps)
- Consider if you need to think about stepping aside from the original goals to work directly with motivation, self-sabotage, learned helplessness, secondary gain or other impediments to progress
- Accept that some clients need longer to adapt to change than others
- Consider if might be in the client's best interests for you to refer them on.

Remember that – for both you and your client – there is no such thing as failure, only feedback.

Clients who don't turn up

The odd client no show is probably the inevitable fate of every business that runs by appointment. Look at those signs in your GP's waiting room about how many patients didn't turn up last week. But for therapists who spend an hour or more with each client, one missed appointment can take a big chunk out of your productivity and income.

GoodTherapy.org cites studies which say that 20-57% of people in therapy do not return after the initial session. Another 37-45% only attend therapy twice, so if your stats are lower than this you may be doing better than you think.

Even so, you might want to put in place a specific method. of dealing with no-shows, which helps things to stay on a professional level, and prevents your annoyance from getting in the way of your rapport with the client.

Why do clients fail to turn up?

There are probably as many answers to this as there are clients who don't show, but we can guess the most likely answers. For example:

- There is a miscommunication between you and the client. Perhaps you and the client have different times or days in your diaries, or your cancellation policy hasn't been made clear
- They genuinely forget, especially likely if there is a long time between appointments, or the appointment is a different time or day from usual
- There's a last-minute emergency or logistical issue, children get poorly, work turns manic so they can't get away, traffic hold-ups cause delays
- The client feels better and doesn't want to continue therapy

- The client doesn't feel therapy is helping and they may be wary of contacting you in case you try to persuade them otherwise
- The client doesn't prioritise therapy or value your time.

Some clients will get in touch if things change, even at very short notice; I had one who emailed me at five in the morning to say she would not be attending her 9 am appointment because she'd been up all night with a sick child and was going to bed. Quite right too, and at least she remembered to let me know.

Others don't. Especially in the case of emergencies they are probably too caught up in their situation to think of contacting you. One lady was run over on the way to her appointment. Thankfully she wasn't badly hurt but she was taken to hospital by ambulance, and I doubt contacting me was high on her list of things to do at that moment!

Others still simply don't seem to think it's important to let you know. A colleague contacted one of his no-shows only to be told: "It's a nice day, I thought I'd do some gardening instead."

How should you respond?

How you deal with no-shows may depend on:

- Whether you pay for your room by the hour, and what the venue's cancellation policy is
- Whether you have a waiting list, made longer by frequent no-shows
- How much it bothers you personally
- Why the client didn't show up (being run over is a pretty good reason)
- How often you get clients generally who don't turn up
- How often this particular client fails to show.

Persistent non-attenders will have to be approached

differently from someone who just misses once (especially if they had a good reason). If a client often fails to show, or turns up late:

- Think about why they have recurring problems getting to appointments. Is it linked to the reason you are working with them? Do they have underlying motivation issues, emotional or physical difficulties leaving the home, etc? If so, you may need to address those before things will improve
- It might help to offer appointments at a different time or on a different day of the week, or to ask them if they can set up a buddy system with a friend who can help them arrive on time
- If you feel the client isn't able to prioritise or value the therapy enough, it may be best for you to part ways. We'll deal with how to do this gracefully later in this section; for now, we'll just say discuss the problem with them directly, and perhaps offer a referral. If the two of you decide to continue, ask them to pay at least a deposit for sessions in advance, even if this isn't your usual approach.

If you get a lot of clients who regularly miss sessions, review your routines and procedures to see if you could send a stronger message that keeping to appointment times is important. It's about setting appropriate boundaries and you can get help in doing this from supervision and reflective practice.

As with many problems, the best option is to prevent the situation from developing if you can. Try to:

- Include a policy about this in your terms and conditions or contract; make sure every client reads it as well as signing it
- Always write down when the next appointment is, and

either ensure the client does the same or give them an appointment card

- Consider a routine text, call or email to remind clients of their appointments, asking them to contact you if they are unable to attend. One study (Sims *et al,* 2012) showed a 25-28% reduction in missed appointments by simply using text-message reminders, and if you use an online booking system this can probably be automated
- Take a non-refundable deposit or full payment when you book an appointment, rather than when it happens, so at least the cost of your room is covered

It is a good idea to have a system to follow if people don't show up, for example:

- If the client is five minutes late, send a text along the lines of: "I have you down for an appointment at [time] today: are you on your way?" As this is friendly and non-confrontational, in genuine cases of delays, misunderstandings, forgetfulness or emergencies they'll get back to you and you can go from there without any impact on your rapport
- If you don't hear from them after 24 hours and you haven't already been paid for the appointment, invoice them, referring back to your terms and conditions
- If this isn't paid, send a reminder which tells them you may take legal action if they fail to pay this time. Whether you finally do this is entirely up to you, sometimes it's easier to just write it off.

Yes, this is tough, but it's fair and professional.

It is likely the client will not want to work with you again if you threaten legal action, but as they have already ignored two reminders that's probably on the cards anyway. I tend to waive non-attendance fees in cases where the client has (once) genuinely forgotten or had a problem on the day, in the interests of maintaining rapport, but many clients offer to pay because they know my official policy.

And a final tip, always have something with you that you can do if a client doesn't show. Brainstorm blog titles, answer some emails, or even just play scrabble on your phone. It will do wonders for your stress levels if you don't feel the time was wasted, and you'll be calm and collected when the next client arrives.

Problems with payments

In my experience, one of the commonest problems in collecting payment from clients for therapists is the unease they feel about asking for money. We join the profession to help others and it can feel mercenary to ask for money for doing so. And some clients make it difficult. So, the first step is to check why you're having trouble collecting your fees.

Therapist problems

If you feel awkward asking clients for money, you can arrange your business so that it doesn't have to change hands in the sessions. Ask people to pay by bank transfer or Paypal before their appointment, although you may need to factor into your prices that this can incur fees.

If even this is difficult for you, you might need to look at your own beliefs. In your previous jobs, perhaps payment and the work you did were separated. Do you value what you do as a therapist? Are you happy the amount you are charging is fair to you and your clients?

If any of this is ringing a bell, try reminding yourself that it's not incompatible to help people and run a successful business. Doctors, lawyers, dentists, and social workers all help people and they all get paid for doing so. If your business folds because of lack of money you won't be helping anyone. Sometimes these reminders are enough, but if not, it's a good idea to bring the subject to supervision

Therapy problems

Now we come to the client who doesn't want to pay or who requests a refund because "the therapy didn't work". We've already looked at why the therapy might not be progressing, now let's focus on whether you should still get paid .

I have a clause in my contract which reads: "I will always do my best to help you achieve a successful outcome to your therapy. However, you understand that an agreement to work on an issue does not guarantee a specific outcome." I say this if clients question it. "Imagine you have been accused of a crime. You hire a barrister. The barrister does their very best, uses every skill at their disposal but the jury finds you guilty. Does the barrister waive their fee?"

The answer, of course, is no. In the same way, you are being paid to act ethically and to use your professional skills in the best way you can to help your clients achieve their goals. If there are barriers to success you can identify and work on them, assuming that your client is willing to do so. But the outcome is dependent on so many factors beyond your control that it's unreasonable to suggest that you are wholly responsible for it. Therefore, unless there are exceptional circumstances do not waive your fee.

Client problems

The final issue around collecting payments is clients who for whatever reason, may fail to pay .

From talking to other therapists, bad debts (clients who fail to pay what they owe) seem to be less of a problem for us than for many other businesses. Most practices have options for clients to pay online or by bank transfer, or accept cash, cheques or cards. In seventeen years of seeing one-to-one clients I have only ever had one cheque that bounced, and that was a genuine mistake. When I dropped her a line to let her know the cheque had been returned, she was mortified and wanted to immediately drive to my home with cash to replace it. We agreed she could bring payment to the next session, which she did (along with a bunch of flowers by way of apology). No big deal.

Corporate non-payers

Digressing for a moment, corporate clients can be a whole different ballgame from one-to-one clients. Most businesses would rather have money in their bank account, and some will wait till the very last minute to pay you. My advice is to set the scene for professionalism right from the start:

- Ask for a deposit when booking any kind of seminar or workshop for a business, if you don't receive it, don't provide the service
- Include a cancellation clause so if you have done all the preparation and they cancel at the last minute, you can still get paid at least part of what was agreed
- Have a written contract which clearly lays out what payments are due and when
- Invoice them immediately you have provided the service, with a 'due by' date clearly shown on the invoice (if you don't seem to care about when you receive the money, why should they?)
- Take action immediately if they don't pay on time (for the same reason).

You might remember the James Herriott books, about a vet in the 1930s Yorkshire Dales? His boss Siegfried claimed to apply a billing system he called PNS – Polite, Nasty, Solicitors – and it's not a bad approach, although I have adapted it a little and interpreted 'nasty' as 'firm'! This is my system:

- A few days after a bill becomes overdue, drop a fairly informal note, or give them a ring, asking if it's been overlooked and asking when payment will be made. In cases of genuine oversight, this is going to upset no-one, and they'll put things right
- If there is no response, or the promised date comes and goes with no payment made, send a more formal, stricter communication saying you are now very

concerned and setting a deadline for payment, maybe 14 days. Mention that you will consider court action if this is not met. Send this one in writing so if things do come to court you will have evidence

- If still nothing, send a "Letter Before Action" which says (using legalistic language) something along the lines of, "If you don't pay within 7 days, I will take you to court and this is the evidence I will show them (that being your contract, invoice, correspondence, etc). I will also be asking for my costs and interest on the amount outstanding, so it is in your best interests to pay now." You need to get this wording exactly right because, if you don't, you may forfeit the right to recover your court costs. The rules do change over time, and there are different approaches for limited companies and sole traders, but you'll find templates for the up-to-date wording online, and even solicitors who will send one for you for a few pounds. Lovetts Solicitors * claim that 86% of people pay up on receiving a Letter Before Action from them, and my own experience (admittedly based on only two occasions) is 100%, although one left it till thirty minutes before the final deadline.
- If all else fails, there is court or mediation. Even within the UK, the rules about this vary depending on where you live so check the gov.uk website for the latest advice.

Businesses generally owe larger amounts than you receive from individual clients, so it's worth making at least some attempt to recover a debt.

* Lovetts Solicitors. 2020. Lovetts Solicitors | Lovetts Solicitors - Letter Before Action. [ONLINE] Available at: https://lovetts.co.uk/uk-debt-recovery/letter-before-action. [Accessed 4 April 2020].

Individuals who don't pay

With individuals, there's a different dynamic and how you approach it might depend more on why payment hasn't been made. However, it's still important to deal with it quickly and professionally, and not to leave things in the hopes that the client will suddenly realise there's a problem and put it right. Don't let the fear of a fuss over money affecting your rapport with them get in the way; feeling upset about not being paid is already affecting your rapport.

Non-payment is a boundary issue because your fee marks the difference between a professional service and a chat with a friend. You'd be uneasy if a client turned up at your home without an appointment and expected you to make time for a cup of tea and a chat about the kids. You should be equally concerned if the client doesn't pay.

Having said that, a friendly, informal first approach by phone, text or email allows a situation like the client I mentioned earlier, who accidentally picked up an old cheque book, to be resolved with no drama and little if any impact on your therapeutic relationship.

If your client has money problems and is genuinely struggling to pay, consider if you can offer some sort of payment plan. It's important to keep the lines of communication open with this option, and to put any arrangement you make with them in writing so that you both know where you are. From a purely business point of view, you should suspend the therapy sessions until the full payment has been received. Whether you do this in real life will depend on how confident you are that the client will pay up eventually, and whether you can afford to provide the therapy free if they don't.

If the client offers non-financial reasons for not paying, such as forgetting or being busy, you will have to judge how to deal with it appropriately. If the client often forgets or gets distracted by other things, explore this with them in the sessions. In this situation, asking for payment in advance and cancelling sessions for which it isn't received would be reasonable , even if it isn't your usual way of working.

Preventing problems with money

In the end, prevention is better than cure. Make it as easy as possible for clients to pay you and, in most cases, you won't have much trouble receiving payment:

- Make sure your client knows how much to pay and how to pay before they come to your first session, for example, by putting it in your appointment letter
- Include payment terms, and the consequences of non-payment, in your client contract or T&Cs
- Consider price reductions for clients who pay for a block of sessions in advance
- Offer a variety of ways to pay: bank transfer, cash, cheque, card, Paypal etc.
- Value the service you offer – act quickly if payments fall behind, and if you invoice after sessions (perhaps to an insurer or other referring agency) then do so promptly
- Discuss non-payment with the client openly and professionally
- Charge a deposit or ask for payment in advance of the sessions from persistent non-payers
- Don't allow yourself to continue providing therapy for someone who isn't paying and has no written agreement to do so in the future

'Difficult' clients

Before you start worrying about my choice of words, I appreciate I am being somewhat contentious just by writing that title. Hence the quote marks. But it still needs a few words of explanation about what I mean by 'difficult'.

According to NLP presuppositions, everybody makes the best decisions they can at the time they make them. People are, therefore, not broken, they are doing the best they can with the choices they see and the resources they believe that they have. If we accept this model – and, broadly, I do – our job, as therapists, is to help them see choices and resources they have but have failed to recognise, or to develop the skills and knowledge they need to access new ones. This model helps us to become very non-judgemental, and we develop the attitude that clients are never deliberately 'difficult', we just need to find the right way to help or engage them.

However . . .

There's a quote, attributed to many different people, that the difference between theory and practice is that in theory there isn't a difference!

In theory, as above, there are no difficult clients. In the real world, situations which are difficult to deal with can arise when working with some clients, even if we stick to our non-judgemental attitudes. So, when I speak of 'difficult clients' I am not attaching that label to the client personally, simply to a situation where difficulties arise in working with them.

This whole trouble-shooting chapter has been looking at some of these situations, if you want to think about it that way. If you have got this far through it, I hope I have answered most of your questions, but I want to finish with a quick tour of some other common issues that might turn up within your practice.

Clients who persistently over-run

When you first start seeing clients it can be difficult to know what you will fit into a session, whether that's half an hour, an hour, or more. Getting the timing right comes with experience, although the nature of therapy means over-running is going to happen occasionally. I never let a client leave the room in tears or very upset, for example, and will stay with them till they are calm even if that means the next person is kept waiting.

But some clients just seem to take more time than your average appointment. As with so many of these problem areas, you have choices about how to deal with this, and it may be that you will deal with different clients differently. However, here are some questions to ask yourself to get you started.

Are you trying to include everything you know in one session?

Therapy is a process and not an event in most cases, and the changes come over time. Work on one aspect of the problem at a time, don't overload the client with a confusing barrage of techniques.

Is the situation very complex, or does the client have multiple issues?

In this case, break things down into their constituent parts, and (unless they are very interlinked) deal with one goal at a time, although you may find that resolving one area has a knock-on effect on others. One of my clients, having resolved a severe phobia, found that within a few months she had the head space and energy to take up a new hobby, lose some weight, and redecorate her house – all things which had been on her 'to do' list for a long time.

Is the client very chatty?

This is probably one of the trickiest issues to deal with because you don't want to break rapport, but it is up to you to keep the session on track. In my years of working with clients, there have been maybe two or three for who I routinely booked an hour and a half instead of an hour because I knew they would need it. I didn't charge extra for these extended sessions, but probably should have done. If I'd been paying for the room by the hour, I'd have had no choice.

The best approach is to start by analysing what the client is talking about and go from there.

If they have plenty to say but it all seems to be relevant to their presenting problem, it can be very difficult to call a halt, but there are a few ways of keeping this within limits:

- Ask the client to keep a diary and send it to you by text or email the day before each session. Not only does this give more time for actual therapy within the session, but it also allows you to look through the information and pull out the elements you want to discuss in more detail
- Ask the client to list the three or five most important observations, changes or events since the last session, so you do not try to cover everything.

On the other hand, if the client frequently veers off at a tangent to chat about things that seem irrelevant to the therapy, gently guide them back to the subject. Sometimes you can do this non-verbally, for example, by slightly withdrawing your attention and putting your pen down if you have been taking notes. At other times you need to be more direct. You could ask: "How do you think that is relevant to [the reason you're here]?" And go from there.

Going off-topic might also be a form of avoidance, the client using the irrelevancies to distract themselves, and you, from a subject they find uncomfortable. Asking something like: "How far do you think it's true that when I ask about [X] you change the subject?" can be the start to a useful conversation. Alternatively, it could be that the boundaries between therapist and friend are being blurred, and that the client is treating the session more as a social visit than therapy. In this case, you could consider if transference or counter-transference are affecting the relationship and deal with it accordingly.

Clients who don't complete tasks at home

First of all, ask yourself – should you be giving clients tasks to do at home at all?

The answer is probably 'Yes' since there is evidence that it improves clients' overall results. Kazantzis (2010), for example, compared CBT clients who were and were not given tasks to do between sessions, and found that on average clients who were reported better outcomes to therapy than those who were not. Thase and Callan (2006) also found that there is: "relatively consistent evidence from correlational studies to conclude that homework adherence is associated with significantly better outcomes". The benefits of giving clients tasks to do at home are:

- you empower the client, therapy is not something done to them while they remain passive, but something that they take an active part in
- it allows them to practise techniques taught in the therapy room in real-world situations

- it improves rapport when the client sees that what you are teaching them helps
- it speeds up and improves results.

So, if your client doesn't complete tasks at home, what can you do? Here are some suggestions:

- Avoid calling it homework, which has negative connotations for many people. In my previous book, *Their Worlds, Your Words,* I suggest the term add-ons. This tends to have positive associations in all sorts of situations, from buying cars to upgrading your computer, where the add-ons are the extra special features everyone wants, but which aren't included in the basic price. You could also refer to foundation, reinforcement or support tasks, or practise, preparation, and exploration
- Don't let the fact that you're expecting them to work on their issue between sessions come as a surprise. Ensure the client knows right from their first contact with you that you will expect them to complete tasks at home and that these are part of, and important to the success of, the therapy
- Make sure clients know why the things you're asking them to do are relevant, and what they should do to help them to achieve success
- Make sure they understand and can remember what they are supposed to do
- Ensure that it's practical for the client to do what you are asking. Discuss with them when and where they will be able to do it. Ask them about any obstacles that have got in the way of them completing the tasks in the past or might do so in the future, and help them to plan for how these can be overcome
- If the tasks proved too difficult, or the client got stuck,

look at how you can help; perhaps chunking them down into smaller or easier steps.

If, despite your best endeavours, the client persistently fails to do anything at home, the best approach is probably to have a frank discussion about how important reaching the therapy goal is to them. We'll pick up on the consequences of this discussion in the next section, when we talk about letting clients go.

Clients you don't want to work with

Sometimes you are approached by a client and you feel you're not the right person to work with them. That's fine, as long as you're not breaking any anti-discrimination laws (see the next section for more details on that one) you are perfectly within your rights to say so and refer them on. But sometimes you want to stop working with a client you're already seeing because irreconcilable differences have arisen. How do you do that?

I'm certainly not suggesting here that the result of meeting any difficulty with clients is to stop seeing them. In most circumstances, it should be a last resort. Ideally, you will work around problems together and go on to a successful conclusion. But, on rare occasions, that just isn't possible. Some of the reasons for making this decision are:

- Contraindications, medical or other issues come to light that weren't obvious at the start of therapy
- You feel someone more experienced, or a specialist, is needed
- You have one of the frank discussions suggested elsewhere in this section about the client's poor timekeeping, failure to pay, frequent no-shows, failure to complete tasks at home etc. and they refuse to consider solutions

- It becomes clear that your personal, moral or religious values and those of the client are at odds and that this is affecting your ability to work with one another
- There is an irretrievable breakdown in rapport, or you feel the client is becoming too dependent on you due to transference, counter-transference, etc.
- You become unwell and are likely to be off work for a long time
- You don't feel safe with the client, for example, because their anger issues manifest in physical or verbal violence directed at you, or the client makes sexual advances.

Those last two reasons will need a different approach from the others, but we'll come back to them in a minute. In all other cases, it's probably best to discuss the situation with your supervisor before taking the final decision to end the therapy. They may see – or help you see – alternatives.

There are, of course, ethical issues to withdrawing therapy from a client part-way through a series of sessions; it can feel like abandonment from their perspective if not properly handled. On the other hand, your job is to do your best for your client whilst keeping both of you safe. Sometimes that means accepting that you're not the right person to help them. If this happens:

- When you broach the subject with the client, be clear and direct.
- Congratulate them on any progress they have made and tell them why you no longer feel you can work with them. Stick to objective facts when giving a reason, and do not heap blame onto the client
- Remain non-judgemental and empathetic if the client is upset or annoyed because you are considering ending therapy
- Speak to most clients personally, although if they are a

frequent no-show this might not be possible. In that case, send a formal letter or email to let them know you are no longer prepared to work with them

- Offer referrals where you can, or offer to help the client find a new and more appropriate therapist
- If you become unwell, a letter or email to the client explaining the situation will probably be enough. Most people understand that this is not your choice and does not reflect on them. Give them an idea of how long you are likely to be out of action and offer them the choice of waiting till you are well, or of being referred to someone else
- If you feel unsafe with a client, your safety is the most important thing and it's best not to discuss ending therapy face-to-face. Having a clause in your contract that gives you the right to terminate therapy if the client behaves inappropriately makes this easier. Send a formal letter, phrased calmly and politely, and do not enter into negotiations about continuing. If the client asks for a referral, either refuse or ensure you find someone who is better placed to deal with their behaviour than you are.

Clients who don't want it to end

It seems fairly predictable that, once they have met all their goals, clients will end therapy and go on their way, but it's not always that straightforward. Some clients are reluctant for therapy to end, and may want to continue booking sessions even after you feel you have helped them as much as you can. Most Codes of Ethics contain some reference to not extending therapy unnecessarily, so how do you define what's necessary?

In the Therapy Loop section of this book, we talked about

how, for clients, the process of therapy can be linear – they resolve their presenting issue and exit therapy – or circular – resolving the presenting issue raises others which take them around the loop again. To be fair, the vast majority of clients are happy to go back to their improved lives once they've achieved what they came to achieve. But for a small number, it's a scary thought to be without you.

Clients might worry about ending therapy sessions for various reasons. These include:

- They like the routine of coming to see you
- They enjoy the experience of hypnosis
- They worry the results won't last once they are on their own
- You are one of few people who seem to support them
- Professional boundaries have been breached or transference is in play, and they think of you as a friend rather than a therapist.

That last is probably a book on its own, and all I will say here is that if this is the problem, you should get advice from your supervisor. However, you can avoid most of the others by preparing the client properly right from the beginning:

- Have definite, measurable goals and monitor progress in some concrete way throughout the therapy
- Regularly point out the improvements they have made
- Encourage the client to practise self-hypnosis or listen to audios at home
- Give the client an idea of how many sessions they are likely to need, even if you make this clear it's just an estimate. If that changes in either direction, discuss it with them openly
- Ensure you include all the ideas covered in the final part of the Therapy Loop on successfully ending therapy, so the client has confidence that they can maintain their

improvements
- Include a focus on wellness in your therapy, as well as solving the presenting issue
- Encourage the client to look at their lifestyle holistically to ensure they have a good work/life balance, healthy habits and good social and emotional support
- Have a mental health maintenance plan they can take with them when they leave.

Dealing with complaints and bad reviews

Finally, we have to come to it. It has always been possible for clients to make a complaint about your service, justified or otherwise, but with the plethora of feedback sites online and the growth of social media, those complaints can now be made far more easily and publicly than they used to be. It's natural to worry about negative public feedback, but remember that no-one can be all things to all people. It's how you deal with these situations that matters.

Fake complaints can be the simpler ones to deal with, at least in public. For example, when I first permitted feedback on the Yorkshire Hypnotherapy Training Facebook page, I got a couple of one-star reviews from people with whom I had never had any previous contact.

Facebook (and most other review sites) now allow you to request that unfair reviews are deleted, but it was a new thing then and they didn't have any mechanism for removal. So, I used the response box to post something along the lines of: "I am sorry you feel our service is only worth one star. However, as far as I can see you have never been in contact with the school or been on one of our courses. If it is us you are trying to review, could you let me know what training you took with us, when, and how you think we could improve our services?"

Of course, none of them ever came back to me. If they had, and the complaint turned out to be genuine, I had remained polite and willing to listen. And if not, anyone reading my response can see that particular review is fake. This kind of idiocy (the fake reviewer's, I mean, not mine) happens, and is unlikely to put off genuine enquiries.

Dealing with genuine complaints seems more straightforward, but there are some things you have to watch out for. In this case, it's best to take things into a private level of communication rather than discuss them in public forums. Apart from anything else, there are confidentiality issues to consider.

The standard advice is to admit the problem and try to put it right, which intuitively seems like a good idea. The CNHC, for example, say in their Guidance on the Duty of Candour that you should explain to the client what has happened, put things right if you can, and offer an apology. However, there can be legal ramifications to doing this because, in law, an apology can be seen as an admission of liability and offering one might void your insurance cover if the complaint ever comes to court.

Even if you shouldn't apologise, it's best to take action immediately. Whether a complaint or bad review from a genuine client is made in a public forum or privately, a prompt acknowledgement will at least show you take your customer care seriously.

Thank the client politely for letting you know about their concerns and say you will respond to them (privately if their complaint is public) as soon as you can. Just that. Avoid admitting fault, getting defensive, arguing the point, or offering explanations, tempting though it might be.

Then check with your insurance what you should say and do. I'd follow their advice closely since, if things do end up in court, they will be involved in your defence. Don't worry too much about this, though, as most issues can be settled quickly between you and your client.

If you think about it, complaints and bad reviews are a good source of feedback. A client who complains to you isn't bad-mouthing you behind your back – and they are allowing you the opportunity to put things right. It's not the kind of feedback you want a lot of, true, but complaints highlight areas where you could clarify your T&Cs or improve your therapy or customer service for future clients, which can only be a good thing.

Section 5 – You and your practice

Getting the most out of supervision

Don’t let your empathy get you down

Questions from the front line

Getting the most out of supervision

Before we jump straight in and start wondering about which supervisor we should see, we need to start by answering the questions – "What is supervision anyway?" And "Why should I bother?"

What is supervision?

This will depend on who you ask, but here are a couple of definitions:

- Meetings with a colleague (or colleagues) to discuss, in confidence, ongoing cases and issues arising from them, and to work through any personal matters that might affect their own position or ability as practising therapists
- Working under supervision means that a counsellor or psychotherapist uses the services of another counsellor or psychotherapist to review their work with clients, their professional development, and often their personal development as well. Supervision is a professional service, rather than a managerial role. The supervisor acts not as a boss, but as a consultant.

So, the goals of supervision are to help your provide an effective service, and ensure your clients get the best results possible.

You'll notice from this that supervision shouldn't be limited to, "Help – what do I do with this client?", nor should it be like being dragged in front of the headteacher for talking in class, where all your weak points and failings are rehearsed. It's meant to be a positive process of review and support, usually by someone more experienced than you if you're at the start of your career and by your peers later on. And although it is, in part, about your work with clients, there are other elements too, most importantly your welfare and your personal and professional development.

There are many theoretical approaches to supervision, just as there are to therapy.

Some supervisors stick to one or the other, most seem to favour a fairly eclectic approach, taking bits and pieces from here and there to suit themselves and their supervisees. In my view, the one which offers you the best guide to what to include in sessions is Proctor's Three Function Model, (2001) which suggests supervision should cover:

- Education (which Proctor calls the "Formative Functions"), which aims to develop your skills and abilities concerning working with clients, and might involve reviewing work you have been doing, giving feedback and help where needed and identifying any areas where further training might be useful
- Support ("Restorative Functions"), which aims to ensure your wellbeing; for example, ensuring you have effective self-care and coping strategies in place, validating your work-related choices and decisions, and dealing with any emotional fall-out you experience from working with certain clients
- Accountability ("Normative Functions") which aims to maintain the safety and effectiveness of your practice in more general ways, for example, checking that you are familiar with the ethical and legal guidelines that apply to your work.

Even if your chosen supervisor doesn't use this exact model Proctor gives you some good ideas about how you can approach supervision, and what you might like to talk about with your supervisor.

How is supervision different from training or therapy?

This is a really good question, because they do seem to overlap. However, I've put together this chart based on one in the Clinical Supervision Training Manual (2002) which I've adapted to reflect the kind of work and supervision undertaken by most hypnotherapists.

	Supervision	Training/CPD	Therapy
Purpose	Work-related support, both practical & emotional; review of professional practice to ensure it is safe, ethical & competent; identify needs for skills/career/business development	To teach new skills; to consolidate and extend existing knowledge; to assess or evaluate those skills	Personal growth; resolving emotional and behavioural issues; development of improved coping strategies; improved self-awareness
Focus	The supervisee, their practice and their clients	The trainee's learning and professional skills	The client, their personal development and goals
Structure and content	Some broad structure, but responsive to changing situations, decided jointly by the supervisor and supervisee	Goal-oriented via pre-published learning objectives; content is planned in advance and chosen by the trainer	Completely flexible, led by the client's changing needs and progress, although techniques are chosen by the therapist
Progress assessment	Co-operation between supervisor and supervisee	Trainer, perhaps peers	Client feedback
Goals	Better professional practice overall, safety and wellbeing of practitioner and their clients	Improved skill and knowledge in the specific areas covered	Replace unhelpful thoughts, feelings or behaviour with more useful responses

Why bother with supervision?

I did say we had to answer this question sooner or later, and the simple answer, if you belong to a professional body, is that they will require it, at least in the early years of your career. But even so, there should be some other reason for the requirement. Few of us want to do something just because we've been told to and finding justification for supervision is not as easy as it sounds.

There is a general assumption that supervision is a 'good thing' for you and your clients, but there are some basic problems with measuring its effects. The methodology is difficult as it would probably mean removing effective therapists from the supervision process to observe whether this has a detrimental effect on them or their clients, or forcing therapists who don't currently do supervision to undertake it and see if it improves things. I'm sure you can see the ethical and practical issues with doing either.

Besides, most of the studies are carried out in clinical situations, where monitoring and measuring are easier, which means they look mostly at nurses and rarely therapists – certainly not hypnotherapists.

And almost all of the studies demonstrate the effects of supervision on the people supervised and not on their clients or patients.

However, if we can make the mental leap of extrapolating from a medical context, there is evidence to show that, "good clinical supervision improves morale and job satisfaction and may prevent stress and burnout" (London Deanery 2012). And Wallbank and Hatton (2011) said that supervision is: "shown to be successful in reducing burnout and stress in health visiting leaders. The process also restored the leaders' capacity to think clearly, producing a positive impact on risk assessment and action."

We're going to talk about why therapists might be particularly susceptible to job-related stress later, but anything that helps you avoid it definitely seems to be worthwhile.

In the meantime, we can say that the effect of supervision is an area that needs a lot more research, but it does seem to have benefits for those undertaking it. And, anecdotally, this is supported by a survey of hypnotherapists I carried out through Yorkshire Hypnotherapy Training in 2015. I should emphasise that it's a small-scale, informal survey, so can't be argued to be typical of the whole hypnotherapy profession, but it did show that:

- 81.13% of 53 respondents undertook supervision of some kind
- 91.89% of 37 respondents disagreed or strongly disagreed that: "supervision is a waste of time and money."
- 78.37% of 37 respondents agreed or strongly agreed that: "supervision is valuable throughout my career".

I hope this at least supports the ideas that supervision can offer more benefits than ticking a box required by your professional body. It can be enjoyable and thought-provoking and group supervision, in particular, can offer a variety of viewpoints that help to refresh your practice.

Most hypnotherapists seem to work primarily with one-to-one clients. We cannot share successes, worry or frustrations from our working day with family or friends because of the need for confidentiality.

The information exchange we have with clients tends to move in one direction to avoid issues around self-disclosure, so it offers little or no opportunities for casual water cooler conversations about last night's TV or the minutiae of everyday life that is possible in most working environments.

Supervision may be the best chance we have to communicate ethically with others in the same situation as we are, to avoid a feeling of isolation and to feel part of a wider community.

Choosing the right supervisor

Hypnotherapists are lucky in that we can choose our supervisors, rather than having them assigned to us.

The professional bodies have lists of people they consider suitably qualified to act as supervisors and my suggestion is to start there. Contact three or four of them; see who seems to be on your wavelength. It's a bit like choosing a driving instructor – they can all get you to your test but you're going to spend a lot of time together in the car so you might as well choose someone you get along with! As you're reaching out, consider the following;

Known or unknown?

Many trainers provide on-going supervision for their graduates, and it's a comfortable feeling to know the person you're working with. But sometimes that can be too much of a safety blanket and it might be better to go outside your comfort zone and work with someone else, to offer a different point of view and help you develop in new ways.

How will sessions be organised?

Do you want to work face-to-face, on the phone or online? If you are willing to use the phone or go online, geography and distance are not important in choosing your supervisor, but being in a room with someone, where it's possible, can be more comfortable for some people. Most supervisors have a contract setting out how they work, and what they cover so make sure you read this thoroughly before signing up. Just a quick personal gripe here – posting on Facebook groups isn't supervision! It may get you lots of ideas or messages of support but can also be confusing, because the people posting don't know you, or the approaches you're familiar with, and come from many different backgrounds and experience levels. My advice is to keep social media more for general questions, networking and CPD; have a supervisor for personal help and support.

Format

One-to-one supervision focuses on you, your clients and your practice. It tends to be responsive and flexible – if you have a client right now you need to talk about, you don't have to wait till the next meeting to get advice.

On the other hand, group supervision is generally cheaper, and allows you to network with other therapists, build up a referral network and/or socialise. It can be a boost to your confidence if someone asks a question you can answer, and some groups have guest speakers at meetings to help expand your knowledge. But they do divide the supervisor's attention between all those who attend so you may not always get all your questions answered.

My advice to my new graduates is to use a mix of both if possible, finding the balance that suits you best.

Peer support or supervision?

Some groups are run as peer support rather than supervision, meaning that there isn't one specific supervisor but those attending are all similar in experience level and essentially supervise one another. These can be wonderful for more experienced practitioners, but if you are all newly qualified the group will almost certainly need someone more experienced on-call to advise about questions the group can't answer between them.

Also bear in mind that, if no-one is in charge, the group may be less focused than you might wish and group dynamics will come into play without anyone being responsible for managing them (which might result in one person dominating proceedings!).

Theoretical approach

Does the supervisor have a specific theoretical approach to supervision, or to working with clients? If they do, does that fit with your preferences and the way you want to work? If not, ask what sort of topics and areas they generally cover in a supervision session and ensure it fits with your needs.

Your preferences here might change as you get more experienced. Often in the first couple of years, you need a lot of support and guidance. As you get more experienced, you might need to be challenged more to ensure you continue to develop your skills and try new things instead of getting stuck in a professional rut.

Personal preference

This is a tricky area to write about, but it's true to say that we get along with some people more easily than with others. Your supervisor will be a therapist and should be able to maintain a professional relationship with you regardless of personality and points of view, just as you do with your clients. This means individual foibles shouldn't interfere too much.

But transference can play a part. Extreme differences of opinion on how to work with clients can cause difficulties as well. If you think this is an issue, consider if you need to choose someone else. Or at least talk to your supervisor about it.

Cost

Costs will vary because supervisors, like hypnotherapists, are generally self-employed and able to set their own prices. Certainly, finances will be a concern, especially when you are newly qualified, but value can be more important than cost, as we saw in the business section of this book. Choose a person you feel will help you grow your practice and provide an effective service rather than the cheapest supervisor you can find.

Confidentiality and recording supervision

Although you will discuss your client work in supervision it's important to consider issues of confidentiality when doing so. Clients you discuss should be anonymised, which means you shouldn't reveal anything about them that might enable your supervisor to recognise them. The best option is to choose a code name for each client – maybe use their initials, first name only (as long as it's not too unusual), or a reference number. Then you can both be sure who you are discussing while maintaining confidentiality. Ensure that you record in your client notes that you have discussed the client with your supervisor, when, what code name you used and what advice was given, so that you can cross-reference your client and supervision records should there ever be a query.

Just as you owe confidentiality to your clients, your supervisor owes it to you. Whatever you talk about in supervision shouldn't go any further, although many supervisors apply a kind of duty of care rule and will break confidentiality in certain circumstances. This should be outlined in your supervisor's contract, or at least made clear to you before you start working with them.

Conclusions

Some hypnotherapists' professional bodies only seem to require you to be in supervision for the first few years of practice, although after that they often use words like "encouraged", so you should check the rules of any groups that you register with. But most professions that are required to undertake supervision – nurses, counsellors, and so on – are obliged to do so as long as they are in practice, and there is nothing to stop you also having a supervisor throughout your career.

Finding the right supervisor is essential, and you may find that you have different supervisors over the years to reflect your changing needs, or for different purposes (one who's focused on business-building and another for client work, for example). That's fine.

Supervision should give you value for the time and money you're investing in it and not become simply a box-ticking exercise. It should help you and your business grow.

Don't let your empathy get you down

Compassion fatigue, also sometimes referred to as "Caregiver Fatigue", "Secondary Traumatic Stress Disorder" or "Vicarious Trauma", is not an illness or a medical condition, it's a reaction to stress characterised by a set of signs and symptoms which happen because of your circumstances, and how effectively you cope with them.

Compassion fatigue varies from other stress-related issues like burnout in that it most often appears in those who help others, provide them with support and/or listen to their upsetting or traumatic stories. Kearney (2009) says that the two conditions can be distinguished because burnout is a response to stressors in the work environment and compassion fatigue, "results from stresses generated between the clinician and the patient's suffering." As Portnoy (2011) puts it: "Compassion fatigue is caused by empathy. It is the natural consequence of stress resulting from caring for and helping traumatized or suffering people."

Clearly, as therapists, we are at risk. Compassion fatigue is thought to have three main elements and it's how they interact that can cause the problems. These elements are:

- Job satisfaction, the joy and positivity you get from doing your job well
- Exposure to risk, how often you are exposed to other people's problems, and how severe or traumatic these are
- Stress levels, partly those from your job (including exposure to risk, above) but also family issues and problems which affect your wellbeing.

Essentially when the three elements are balanced, things are pretty good and you have all the resources you need to cope with the demands that life has placed upon you. But if your pleasure in helping people is undermined for some reason, or your risk or stress levels increase, there is an imbalance. Over the short term, this might be manageable, but if it persists, it will start to impact both your physical and emotional health.

Symptoms of compassion fatigue

These can include:

- Physical and emotional exhaustion or feeling overwhelmed
- Sadness, anxiety, fearfulness, depression, anger
- Poor concentration, memory and/or sleep patterns
- Feelings of detachment and/or persistent negativity
- Physical illness, such as headaches
- Avoidance of situations we perceive as being difficult to cope with
- Irrational feelings or a tendency to cry where you wouldn't have done before.

If you are a therapist who deals with stressed, depressed or anxious clients, you'll probably recognise this list. What it shows is that you are not immune to the pressures and stressors that affect your clients. Accept it. You are only human.

Risk factors for compassion fatigue

Those most at risk are:

- Perfectionists
- Those who consistently put the needs of others before their own
- Those who have low levels of social support
- Those who have high levels of stress in their personal lives
- Those in the caring professions.

Although I couldn't find any specific figures for hypnotherapists, we can include them in the caring professions. Studies tell us that up to 85% of healthcare workers, 25% of ambulance paramedics, 34% of hospice nurses, and 72% of mental health professionals working with Hurricane Katrina victims suffered anxiety or other symptoms of compassion fatigue*.

If you feel you may have compassion fatigue (or if you are a supervisor who is worried about one of your supervisees) there are a couple of self-assessment protocols which are freely available online. Search for ProQOL5 (the Professional Quality of Life scale) or the Compassion Fatigue and Satisfaction Self-Test for Helpers.

Prevention and cure

As you might have guessed, there is no cure as such for compassion fatigue, but stress management and relaxation techniques plus effective self-care programmes help in reducing and preventing the symptoms. These include breathing exercises, guided meditation, self-hypnosis and exercise, along with firm professional boundaries and an effective support network.

Of course, having an effective support network when you offer a confidential service to your clients can be tricky. You can't come home and unload about your day to your family or friends, as most people can. In this context, a support network has to be professional, and that means good supervision and peer support throughout your career. Supervision is often thought of as the place where you go

* Wikipedia Contributors (2019). *Compassion fatigue*. [online] Wikipedia. Available at: https://en.wikipedia.org/wiki/Compassion_fatigue. [Accessed 11 May 2020].

when you don't know what to do, but, as I've discussed earlier, it should also (among other things) ensure that you have self-care protocols in place and that they are working.

Tips to avoid and reduce compassion fatigue:

- Be aware of how you're feeling and accept that you might sometimes need help
- Be willing to seek out therapy yourself if you are struggling
- Eat a healthy diet; planning and preparing meals in advance can help you avoid the takeaways
- Monitor your smoking, alcohol intake and any other unhealthy tendencies!
- Make time for you; engage in activities that you enjoy every week; take time out for a bubble bath or meditate, schedule regular social time in your diary
- Look for practical solutions to difficult situations and put them in place; get help with this if you need it
- Recognise your stress triggers, at home and work, and how they interact
- Know your limits. It's OK to say no, whether that's referring on a client you don't feel is a good fit or getting someone else to clean the house or walk the dog
- Therapy tends to be a sedentary job so make sure you exercise regularly; park a bit further away from work and walk in, join a gym, yoga class or sports club, play in the park with your kids, take the stairs instead of the lift if your therapy room is not on the ground floor
- Get up and move around between clients; do a few stretches or allow time for a short walk a couple of times a day
- Get support; peer or networking groups and a good supervisor will offer support about work without

confidentiality issues and making the effort to keep in touch with friends by email, text, phone or in person will help with the personal side of things

- Aim for excellence, not perfection. There's absolutely nothing wrong with having high standards or seeking to improve things, but accept that now and then you need to give yourself a break
- Be realistic about how many clients you can help at times when your stress levels at home are high, and vice versa
- Don't be the worst boss you ever had! Take time off; just as you would if you worked for someone else. Book regular holidays from work (even if you don't go away) and ensure you have at least one day off per week
- Use the good advice you'd give to a client in your situation.

If you already have a self-care routine, review it regularly to ensure it's still working for you. If you haven't been doing any self-care at all you can't possibly integrate all these ideas in your life overnight. That would be stressful in itself!

Start with one or two, pick the ones that look easiest to get you going. Once the new habit is established, choose and add another idea, until you are in a routine that supports and nourishes you.

Questions from the front line

I wanted this book to address the real world concerns therapists have, so for the big finale. I sent out a plea for questions and these are some of the ones that came back. Thank you so much to all those who contributed.

Like anyone attempting an Agony Aunt role, I have limited information to put the questions in context and sometimes, the best response I can give is that it depends on the specific circumstances. I can, however, at least offer suggestions about how to start finding your own ideas, advice, and support.

One option is, pretty much always, your supervisor, but as I don't want to trot that out in every answer, I'm dealing with it here. (Plot exposition again, perhaps.)

We've already discussed how getting the right support from supervision and asking questions about the things that bother you is essential. This applies even if you're concerned that your questions might seem petty or silly. If these questions are worrying you, they're not either of those things.

Try not to worry about being judged; a good supervisor would much rather you asked a question than worried or made a mistake, and is 100% unshockable (a bit like you when your clients express concerns about telling you things).

If you do feel your supervisor is overly critical it can be good to discuss it within your sessions. Transference may be an issue, or perhaps your styles of giving and receiving feedback aren't working well together.

And if your question isn't covered here, feel free to drop me a line via social media or through the website. I will do my best to help.

Therapist Confidence: "Am I losing my touch?"

A common situation is when a therapist finds a technique they have used a lot has not worked on recent clients. They then ask if they are losing their touch.

My answer is: "Probably not, but it would be a good opportunity to reflect on whether you are relying too heavily on one technique, or limiting your flexibility in the way you work with clients."

A lot is said and written about being responsive to your client's needs, building in their experience and interests. Quite rightly too, but it's also true that the therapist being confident in what they're doing is important. Plus, for some issues, you might follow a specific protocol which lays down what to do session by session, either because it's the way you have been taught, or because it has some evidence behind it to show that it works. So, re-using techniques as a general principle is not an issue.

However, that doesn't mean that you should become what's often called a 'cookie-cutter' therapist (providing sessions which all have exactly the same size and shape) or lose your ability to go off-piste if the situation requires it.

Start with this. Each client's problem is unique to them, whether it's anxiety, a phobia, a desire to quit smoking, lose weight or anything else. Yes, two people with the same presenting issue might have factors and symptoms in common but their social, emotional and psychological landscape is their own and provides a unique context within which they experience their problem. That makes it unlikely that they will require the same approach to resolve it.

Focus on the client in front of you and set aside what they have in common with other clients with similar issues. What is this particular client doing, feeling or thinking? How does their problem fit with other areas of their life? What meaning do they attribute to it, and what words do they use to describe it? That should come first, and your choice of how to help them improve things – whether technique-based or off the cuff – comes second.

You might find TOTE useful when you are planning your sessions. This is a model of problem-solving behaviour developed in 1960 by Miller, Gallanter and Pibram* and stands for Test, Operate, Test, Exit.

TOTE gives you a framework of checking whether what you're doing is working, and it can be used as part of reflective practice. You can see how it works on the next page.

* Encyclopedia Britannica. (n.d.). George A. Miller | American psychologist. [online] Available at: https://www.britannica.com/biography/George-A-Miller#ref1200618. [Accessed 22 May 2020].

	General structure[c]	Applied to your clients
Test	Test for incongruities.	Get a representation of the problem in the here and now - symptoms, triggers etc.
Operate	Intervene to remove the incongruity.	Apply a therapeutic intervention aimed at resolving the client's issue.
Test	Test to see if the incongruity is still there.	If the problem wasn't resolved, go back to 'operate'. Apply a different intervention and test again.
Exit	Once the incongruity is eliminated, exit the process.	End therapy when the problem is resolved.

It comes across as a kind of formalised trial and error process, but remember that your trials (interventions) are based on your knowledge, skills and experience as a therapist; you are not (should not be) randomly throwing techniques at the client in the hopes that something will change. Each test will help you identify what doesn't work for your client and take you a step further to finding out what does. Flexibility is important and although many techniques do lend themselves to different situations or can be adapted to suit different clients, your ultimate goal is not to apply a 'one size fits all' approach to therapy but to respond to the needs of the client in front of you.

Closing the deal: "This week I had three enquiries which did not lead to bookings, am I doing something wrong?"
Do you remember the section earlier in this book on learned helplessness? We showed then that it can take as little as three failures to kickstart that reaction and it might be playing a part now in making you worry.

You can use reflective practice on these enquiries to help you discover if you can improve your way of answering them, or take some other action, or if it is just a random cluster. Look critically at those enquiries and ask yourself:

- Have you been answering questions as you usually do, or have you been busy, disorganised, rushed or distracted?
- Have you felt increasingly desperate to sign clients up with each failure, and might that have come across in the way you dealt with people?
- Is your conversion rate (the number of clients who sign up after making an initial enquiry) always lower than you'd like?

If you have answered 'yes' to any of these questions, you

might benefit from polishing your approach to answering enquiries. Here are some useful principles:

1. Only respond to enquiries when you have plenty of time to spend answering a client's questions.
2. If your personal life is intruding, consider if you need to take a break from client work.
3. Aim to approach each enquiry by focusing on how you can help this particular person, without considering how many clients you have or need at present, finances, or other similar factors.
4. Have a checklist, to ensure you have covered everything in responding to an initial enquiry. You don't want to come over like an automaton but having a short guide can be handy.
5. Therapy talk and concepts are your everyday life, but they may be way out of your client's comfort zone. Avoid using jargon, and spend more time on what you can help them do than on explaining the theory behind your therapy.
6. End your responses, whether on the phone or by email, with a call to action, which means explaining exactly how to take the next step to access your services.
7. Consider acquiring some non-manipulative sales training as part of your CPD, to help you answer customer queries in the right way.

Once you have absorbed that, there are some other questions about how you deal with enquiries which you should look at:

- Have all those who made the enquiries found your details the same way?
- Are these enquiries different in any way from the ones you usually get?

If you have answered 'yes' to these questions, you may need to review your advertising to help you attract enquiries from clients who are better suited to work with you. Create a profile of your ideal client; present your information in a way they will respond to and place it where they are likely to see it.

The final question I would encourage you to ask is:

- Do you know the reasons people haven't signed up for therapy?

If you do, especially if everyone gave the same reason, is it something you could address? Having thought in advance about responses to the most common objections raised by potential clients means you don't have to think on the spot.

Even if they give different reasons, think about what you said in your responses. Did you talk about value, for example, or price? The history and mechanics of your therapy, or what you could help them achieve? Yourself, or them?

If none of these questions gave you any insight, you have more than likely been on the end of a run of bad luck. We all get these.

Try tracking your enquiries and bookings over time, so you know what your usual conversion rate is. Your confidence will be maintained by seeing that for every week where no-one signs up with you, there are other weeks where everyone does.

Professional reputation: "How do I deal with unwelcome praise?"

Not all praise is good praise. Here is an example of a common issue. Someone wrote to me asking: "An ex-client, who came to me for weight loss and actually put on more weight is on Facebook and praising me. She says seeing me was fun. I don't think this is doing my business any good, what can I do?"

I do understand, it must be frustrating if you feel you are being praised for the wrong reason.

There is a mechanism on most social media to have posts and reviews removed if you feel they are unfair but as what she's saying is positive, I suspect all you can do in this case is find a reframe for yourself to change how you feel about her actions.

As I'm sure you know, a client's presenting issue isn't always the issue they need to deal with. Sometimes it's a symptom of an underlying problem, or even just a reason to get them in through the door until they feel comfortable enough to discuss what's really bothering them.

If any of this lady's friends contact you as a result of her posts you will be able to explain that they are individuals whose situation is unique, and that you would approach their therapy accordingly. Or, if all they want from you is some pleasant time out from a busy life, maybe you could open up your services and offer a one-off, fun relaxation session for a fixed fee?

The fact is that although this lady presented with weight issues and they didn't resolve, she clearly got what she needed from the sessions. She calls this process 'fun', but perhaps what you could call it is 'me time', 'relaxation', 'confidence' or even 'self-esteem'. And there is nothing wrong with that.

Ethical Dilemmas: "How do I work within my competence and my preference?"

I have been asked to work outside of my competence

Being asked to operate outside of your sphere of expertise is an issue which comes up from time to time.

Here is an example: "A client wants me to see her 10-year-old son. I have no experience in treating children and would rather refer on, but she is insisting it is me or nothing. What should I do?"

There are two main elements to this question. One is whether you want to see your client's child, and the other is whether you should. Let's start with whether you should, because that might decide for you, regardless of your personal preferences.

Firstly, you say you have no experience in treating children but it's not clear whether you have the training to work with children and have simply never used it, or if you lack relevant training. If the latter, you have to refer this child on.

If you do have the training, you need to think about whether this is the right opportunity to use it. Do you have everything you need in place to work with children? For example, although it's not a legal requirement for most self-employed therapists, your professional body or insurance may prefer you to have a DBS (Disclosure and Barring Service) check before you take on clients who are minors. Do you have one?

Have you considered the potential pitfalls of seeing two people from the same family at the same time? Many of these can arise regardless of whether one of the potential clients is a child.

- Working with this child specifically would create a dual relationship with Mum, who would see you sometimes as a client and sometimes as the mother of a client. At times, there could be conflict or overlap between these roles
- Unless you are trained in family therapy, you will need to keep the two sets of sessions separate, but what if

Mum wants to discuss her son's progress in her sessions, or vice versa?

- Even with separation, confidentiality issues can arise. Mum might tell you in her session that she is struggling to cope with how upset her son is about an incident at school. Because you were told that in her session, you can't use the information in the son's therapy, or allude to it in any way, unless he tells you about it as well. He might not
- It's easy to slip and accidentally reveal your knowledge of something like this that you are not supposed to know to one or other of your clients. Your record-keeping must be exemplary and detailed to ensure this doesn't happen
- And finally, according to Dianne Schetky (2001), a kind of rivalry can grow up between your two clients as each of them expects you to be on their side, and your ability to be empathetic and non-judgemental to both if they disagree on a subject may be severely tested.

It's not impossible to get around these pitfalls, therapists do it all the time, but if you don't feel able to do so, you need to refer on.

If practicalities are not the problem, you need to think about what is. Is it that you don't want to work with any children, or just this one? Do you just need a boost to your confidence about working with children? Is it the nature of the issue that the son has? Would you be more open to working with him once Mum is no longer your client?

Be honest with yourself but, in the end, if you don't want to work with the son (whatever the reason) it is almost certainly better that you don't. Your reluctance might translate into resentment, pre-judgements, and lack of empathy, none of which will help your relationship with your current client. This means you need a way to present a refusal to Mum that doesn't break the rapport you have with her. Honesty, combined with tact and diplomacy, is your best way forward.

Schedule a bit of time to talk to her about this, preferably outside her sessions. Thank her for her trust in asking you about helping her son and say why you can't. I would avoid subjective explanations based on your personal preference, which could be misconstrued. Instead, offer a short, practical reason: your lack of training or experience; concerns about confidentiality, or simply say it is not your policy to work with two members of the same family. Stand firm and don't argue the point.

Ask Mum how she chose you as her therapist. What was it about you that made her pick up the phone? It could be your experience or qualifications, the way your personality came over on your website, or a referral from someone she trusted. Whatever it was, she decided that you were the right person for her, and you can suggest that it's just as important to find the right fit for her son. Offer to help her do this; make a referral to a specific therapist if you can or offer advice on finding one.

If Mum still says that she would rather he didn't see anyone else, don't let this pressure you into changing your mind. You've made the best decision, both for yourself as a therapist and for the son as a potential client. Simply reassure her that if she changes her mind in the future, you will be happy to help her find someone suitable.

I'd prefer to see only women as clients. Can I do this?

This is a question I am often asked by students about to graduate, especially if they are women living alone who plan to work from home.

Usually, the reason given is that they wouldn't feel safe inviting unknown males into their home.

It is important to think honestly about why you have this preference. Are you generally uncomfortable around men, or only as therapy clients? Is there an experience in your past which makes you wary of being alone with men? Is your preference based in your personal fears, anxieties or experiences?

If the issue lies with you, I strongly advise you to chat with your supervisor, or even see a therapist of some sort and work it through. We don't have to be perfect to practise as therapists, but it's definitely wiser to get the larger issues sorted rather than allowing them to impact on the way you work. However, even if practicalities like personal safety are at the heart of your preference, you need to look at both ethics and the law before definitely deciding to see women only.

Most professional bodies acknowledge the importance of both elements. Look on the next page at these two examples from the respective Codes of Ethics of two UK hypnotherapy bodies.

	The NCH[cii]	The GHR[ciii]
On keeping within the law	Discrimination includes allowing your belief of a client's protected characteristic (age, disability, gender identity, marriage and civil partnership, pregnancy and maternity, race, religion or belief, sex, and sexual orientation) to influence the standard of care you provide.	[You must] act in a non-biased, non-prejudicial manner towards all clients, providing those clients with an identical quality of service and treatment irrespective of the many differences which are to be found between clients, including but not restricted to: race, gender, sexual orientation, disability etc.
On keeping safe/providing your service	You must not do (or omit to do) anything or allow anything to be done by others under your instruction which could put your client or another associated person at risk of harm.	Practitioners should give full consideration to the efficacy of treatment, including the manner in which their rapport with the client may affect such efficacy.

Based on this, if you feel strongly that inviting people of a specific gender into your home would put you at risk of harm, or that concerns over safety would affect your ability to build rapport and provide effective therapy, you could argue that you could ethically see only female clients. But, legally, you still need to avoid anything that would be considered discriminatory behaviour.

The main piece of relevant legislation in the UK is the Equality Act (2010) which makes it illegal to discriminate against people falling into categories called protected characteristics. There are nine of these, but the one that is of interest here is sex, which refers to: "a male or female of any age . . . using the commonly-accepted words man and women".

If you want to restrict your service based on one of the protected characteristics, you need to be able to show that (a) you have a good reason to do so other than discrimination, and (b) that there isn't a less discriminatory way to resolve your concerns.

There are several situations listed in the Act (para 27 of Schedule 3) which it suggests would constitute good reasons:

- It's a gender-specific service
- A combined service would be inadequate, or less effective
- There is an imbalance of demand for the service and it is not practical to provide for both sexes (e.g. a local authority provides a battered women's refuge but not an equivalent for men because there is not enough demand to make it viable)
- Separate services are provided where service users need special care (e.g. in a hospital)
- Service users might object to the presence of the opposite sex (e.g. in changing rooms or toilets)

- Physical contact is involved and those using or providing the service might reasonably object if the other person is of the opposite gender (the Act gives the example of a female mobile massage therapist who may not feel comfortable massaging men in their own homes).

The Citizens Advice Bureau also suggests that health and safety considerations or the welfare of the individuals concerned would be an adequate reason, so perhaps a formal risk assessment would be a good start and would also prove you have considered other alternatives if your policy was ever queried.

You also need to consider what you would do if you were approached for therapy by someone who does not see themselves as part of a simple male/female dichotomy, for example, a gay, non-binary or transgender person, especially since these are also protected characteristics. On the latter, the Equality and Human Rights Commission says; "generally, a business which is providing separate services or single-sex services should treat a transsexual person according to the sex in which the transsexual person presents (as opposed to the sex recorded at birth), as it is unlawful to discriminate against someone because of gender reassignment. Where a transsexual person is visually and for all practical purposes indistinguishable from someone of their preferred gender, they should normally be treated according to their acquired gender unless there are strong reasons not to do so."

Overall, then, it's complicated.

If you want to restrict your clientele to one gender you need to establish both legally and ethically acceptable reasons to do so. My recommendation is to check with a legal advisor and your professional body before advertising that you offer a single-sex service.

Of course, specialising in female issues, or simply branding your service in a way which is likely to appeal to women is fine, as is placing advertisements where women are most likely to go. You just need to plan ahead for how you will respond to enquiries that come from anyone who doesn't fit your 'ideal client' profile.

Your wellbeing as a therapist: "How do I keep a good work/life balance?"

Work life balance and burnout

Getting the balance right between work and life is not easy and many therapists worry about this, especially when they are new. A typical worry would be: "I have been seeing six clients a day and am finding it difficult to switch off. Is this too many?"

This is very much a "how long is a piece of string" question, since different therapists are comfortable seeing different numbers of clients. But if you are finding it difficult to switch off, it probably does indicate that you need to work differently, either in the way you work with clients or the number of clients you see.

It's very easy, especially when you first set up in practice, to take any and all clients who contact you, and to re-arrange your schedules around their preferences for appointment times. You tell yourself you are only doing this until the business gets off the ground, but you are setting a precedent, and it's hard to get out of the habits when you are more established.

The following points are designed to help you set your personal limit on client numbers:

- Identify exactly what's making it hard to switch off – is it your clients' situations or worries about your ability to help them? Is it all clients or specific ones?

- What sort of clients and issues do you work with? If the work you do involves listening to many distressing stories, have a look at the section on compassion fatigue earlier in this book. It may be the type of clients you are seeing rather than the number that is causing difficulties in switching off
- How many days a week do you currently see clients? And how often do you see six in a day?
- How much job satisfaction do you get from seeing clients? Would specialising be a good idea, or perhaps removing certain issues from your list of services?
- Realistically, how many hours can you devote to your therapy business each week? When?
- How many of those hours will be spent on admin, preparation, CPD, PR etc?
- Can you afford to delegate any of these tasks to free up some time? (I look at all potential costs in terms of how many client hours I will have to work to raise the money.)
- What other calls on your time are there? (Job, family, self-care etc.) How much time do these need?
- How confident are you in your training and skills? (The more confident you are, the better you will probably cope.)
- How experienced are you? (The more preparation and reading you need to do before each session, the less time you have to be with clients.)
- What sort of income do you want from your therapy business? What makes it viable?
- Does your fee allow you to raise this much in the time you have available?

To put this in perspective, a poll run by the Sensitive Therapist website showed that 74% of respondents said that fourteen clients a week or less was their ideal, with only 2%

wanting to see twenty or more. And a 2004 study on therapist burnout said that not only is a high caseload a factor in your mental health, it was also the second most important factor in determining poor client outcomes. So, seeing fewer clients can make you a more successful therapist.

My tips for taking control of your client hours are:

- Schedule an admin day each week; don't try to fit these tasks in around your clients
- Set specific days and times for seeing clients and stick to them
- If, occasionally, you choose to make an exception, charge an out-of-hours fee which is significantly higher than usual. I've found people make more effort to attend within my set hours when I mention this
- Run a waiting list if you have more clients than you can see in a week instead of extending your hours
- Prioritise good self-care and support and don't see them as optional extras
- Take on clients you are confident you can help, bearing in mind your training and experience levels
- Delegate non-client aspects of running your business where you can
- Raise your prices – you may get fewer clients, but they will be the ones who really want to work with you and your income will remain the same.

How much self-care do I need?

As a therapist, you'll be used to metaphors, so in this instance think of life as a plate-spinning act – I'm sure you've seen these. A performer has several tall, thin, bendy poles on which he, or she, balances (allegedly) ordinary dinner plates. The skill is in keeping each plate spinning fast enough to stay on the top of its pole, instead of falling to the floor in a heap of broken china. According to Wikipedia the World Record for this, set in 1996, is one hundred and eight plates spinning at one time.

In this metaphor, the different plates represent different demands placed on you. There's one for clients; one for running your business; one for your other job (if you have one); one for the family; one for your own needs, and so on. A healthy level of self-care is what enables you to comfortably keep all the plates spinning.

Because this is entirely personal and circumstantial (you may need more self-care at some times than others) it's tricky getting it right, but you can perform a self-care audit to see how things are going. Dr Joanie Connell, President of Flexible Work Solutions, Inc. suggests it's all about getting a good work-life balance and developed the following questionnaire to help you check if you're getting it right.

Answer true or false to the following:

1. My life and work demands often interfere with each other.
2. Someone else has control over my work schedule.
3. It's a struggle to get time off from work when I need to.
4. I spend a lot of time responding to personal emails and phone calls when I am at work.
5. I don't have time to exercise at least three times a week.
6. I have had to give up most of my hobbies.
7. I sleep less than eight hours per night on a regular basis.
8. I have frequent headaches and/or stomach aches.
9. I catch myself making mistakes on the job often.
10. It is important to check my phone and email when I leave work.
11. It is hard to shift my focus of attention to the issue at hand.

12. I find myself worrying about how I'll get everything done.
13. I work more than 40 hours a week.
14. It's hard not to be irritable and lose my temper.
15. I don't have enough time to relax.
16. I frequently have to deal with work emergencies when I am not there.
17. I am tired all the time.
18. My family and friends are routinely upset at me for not being available to them.
19. I am often needed outside of work during work hours.
20. I drink more than three cups or shots of caffeinated drinks per day.

The more you said, 'true', the more likely you are to be at risk from stress-related issues. The more 'false' replies you gave, the better. The healthier your work-life balance is, the more likely you are to be getting the right amount of self-care.

How can I incorporate regular self-care into my routine without feeling guilty?

We've talked about self-care a lot in this book, but this is one aspect of it that we haven't really covered, as yet. Those of us who take up therapy for a profession tend to have a strong desire to help others, but we can come to believe that this is not compatible with taking care of ourselves. This belief can come from a number of places including:

- You assume that putting yourself first is always selfish, whatever the circumstances
- You feel you should be doing something else (for family or work)
- You assume that others will criticise you for prioritising yourself
- You feel that using time and energy for self-care reduces your ability to care for others or to be successful

- You haven't got firm professional boundaries, and feel it's wrong to switch off from work
- You were taught as a child that you should always put the needs of others first
- You feel undeserving of self-care, perhaps because of issues with self-esteem.

You'll need to address the particular reasons you feel guilty to truly embrace self-care and get the most out of it, but essentially you need to work on boosting your self-care capacity. That means accepting that it's OK to balance your own needs – physical, emotional, psychological, spiritual and professional – with those of other people, and to sometimes make choices that benefit you instead of them.

Benefiting yourself means your self-care should be based on your own needs and preferences, and not what others tell you it should be. Just as we can't provide 'one size fits all' therapy, we can't provide 'one size fits all' self-care. I asked around to see what therapists did for self-care activities and here are just a few of the answers.

Norma: I take regular breaks throughout the working day e.g. a short walk, being around nature, being mindful of our five senses.

Janie: I take time out to sculpt and sketch. I have never been one to self-groom or go on shopping trips, so creativity is my self-care, where I get to lose myself, my thoughts and just focus on the next chisel or pencil mark. Heavenly.

Michelle: self-care for me is a lovely nap! Nothing like it – it is totally refreshing and resets me.

As you can see, they're all different. You know from your work with clients that stress is all about the perception of a situation and so is self-care. Jumping off a bungee tower, hosting a party for five-year-olds or even gardening can be a chore or a pleasure depending on your point of view. If self-care is a chore it will simply be another task you should be doing and won't achieve its aims at all. You may even end up feeling guilty about failing to do it!

Khristi Pahr cites Dr Perpetua Neo: "If you find yourself obsessing over the 'correct way' to self-care, and feel like crap consistently after it, then it's a big sign to stop." And when it makes you feel good, that will help you let go of the guilt.

How do I balance being empathetic with being an effective business-person?

Empathy is being able to understand and share the feelings of someone else, and it's not perhaps the first thing you think of when you consider the leading lights of business. In the TV programme *Dragon's Den*, for example, even the title of the programme is designed to make you think of the business gurus as fierce, dangerous and scary.

There is a growing interest in empathy in business, since it is said to help managers relate to the people they're managing, respond to their social environments and build useful, trust-based networks. The downside of this is that it can also get in the way of making logical decisions, which is an important part of running a business.

A study at Yale University (2016) asked two groups of people to listen to a child describing his pain and then to make a decision about whether to move him higher on a medical priority list. They were aware that, if they did this, other people judged by doctors to be more urgently in need of treatment would have to wait longer.

Two-thirds of those who were asked to empathise with the child moved him higher, even though it was against medical advice, and only one-third of those asked to make an objective assessment did so. Which is perhaps why empathy and practical business decisions don't always mix.

Modern research suggests that there are three different kinds of empathy:

- Cognitive empathy, also called perspective-taking, which includes understanding what someone is feeling and why, but not necessarily feeling it with them
- Affective empathy, which is about understanding someone's emotional state and feeling with them
- Compassionate empathy, which motivates you to take appropriate action to help the other person.

Most therapists have no problem applying affective and compassionate empathy. It's usually a natural inclination, encouraged by our training. But it can also lead to increased risk of burnout and compassion fatigue, difficulties in separating home and work, and trouble making the more objective business decisions.

This is especially true in areas like charging a fair price for what you do, limiting your working hours, collecting unpaid fees, saying 'no' when you need to, and maintaining professional boundaries.*

Cognitive empathy allows you to stand back a bit further. You still understand the other point of view, and how the person is feeling, but you don't have to share it and can,

* Professional boundaries are the rules we apply that define our relationships with clients. They cover things like how (and how often) clients can contact us between sessions, whether touch is acceptable within therapy (e.g. is it OK for your clients to give you a hug?), the limits of confidentiality, the acceptance of gifts, the management of issues like transference and sexual attraction, and what contact we might agree to have with clients on social media. Some boundaries are written into our client contracts or Codes of Ethics, and others are simply implied. Many are flexible and dependent on circumstances (see, for example, our discussion earlier in this book on therapist self-disclosure) but some are absolutely fixed.

therefore, apply your executive decision-making skills more effectively in dealing with the situation. Let's take the example of a client who constantly phones you out of hours for reassurance.

Using affective or compassionate empathy, you feel their need for comfort and want to do something about it. It's extremely difficult not to drop everything you are doing and talk to them. On the other hand, cognitive empathy allows you to understand their need, and why they have it, but to balance that rationally against the fact that it's out of hours, unpaid, and your family deserve some of your time and attention. You may still sometimes answer the phone, but it's a choice and not an obligation.

Most successful business leaders emphasise cognitive empathy over other kinds. It allows them to balance creating a positive working atmosphere and good working relationships with making logical executive decisions. As a therapist you may well work alone, so your working relationships are not quite the same as if you were heading a multi-million-pound conglomerate, but increasing your cognitive empathy will still improve your ability to use your executive skills and help you run your business more effectively.

So, the answer to this question is that you can be effective in business and empathetic, but you need to ensure that you're using the right kind of empathy.

Appendix One: Additional Resources and my other websites

As you've been working your way through this book, or maybe just dipping in and out of it, you'll have noticed references to some free downloads. These are:

- A bonus article
- The Therapy Loop – a full colour, detailed diagram
- A template for Therapy Plans
- A template letter to doctors to use if your client has possible contraindications, which you can add your practice details to
- A medical referrals flow chart to help you decide what to do in each case
- A template Reflective Practice document

Some these are unique to the downloads, if the format of this book didn't allow us to include them, the others appear in the text or appendices but downloading them in usable format means you don't have to copy-type them from the book!

To access these, please go to

https://hypnotherapists-companion.co.uk

Click on 'downloads' in the main menu, then enter the password downloads-please in the box.

All will be revealed!

My other websites:
https://theirworlds-yourwords.co.uk/ - about Their Worlds, Your Words (book)

https://cpd.expert/ - CPD for therapists already in practice

https://www.yorkshirehypnotherapytraining.co.uk/ - multi-accredited Foundation and Practitioner level training for those at the beginning of their hypno journey

https://hypnotherapytrainingblog.blogspot.com/ - online magazine from which inspiration for this book was drawn
https://debbiewaller.com/ - Debbie's therapies

If you have enjoyed this book, please remember to leave a review on Amazon.

Appendix Two: behavioural psychology

I said in the article on aversion that I would give a few more details for those interested in behavioural conditioning. Behaviourism has been around a long time, so this is still quite a quick tour of the ideas, but if you are interested in learning more, there is plenty of reading and courses to be had online.

Behaviourism came about, at least in part, as a response to analytical approaches to psychology developed by people like Freud. Some people felt that these were too heavily reliant on theoretical constructs such as the unconscious mind, the id, ego and super-ego and wanted to take psychology in a more systematic and scientific direction. Therefore, behaviourists are interested in measurable, observable, predictable behaviour and try to avoid having any reliance on introspection or internal processes.

Behaviourists believe that babies are born with a mind empty but ready for conditioning – they called this the 'tabula rasa' or 'blank slate'. All behaviour, according to this theory, is learned.

Behaviourism itself has nothing to do with therapy. It's an approach to understanding how animals (and people) learn by interacting with their environments. However, the principles can be applied to therapy.

Behaviourists refer to 'conditioning' when talking about how behaviours develop because 'learning' implies some sort of internal cognitive process. There are two main kinds of conditioning.

Classical Conditioning

This refers to conditioning which takes place by pairing

something in the environment with a particular response.

There are three stages to classical conditioning, and we can look at them via a famous example – Pavlov's dogs. Pavlov was not a psychologist but a physiologist interested in salivation in dogs and had devised a way of measuring their saliva when they were fed. He predicted that they would salivate when presented with food but was surprised to notice that it also happened when something happened that indicated they were about to be fed – hearing the footsteps of his assistant, for example.

Step one – the unconditioned state

To begin a process of classical conditioning you need a subject (an animal or person), an environmental stimulus (trigger) that will evoke a response, and something to condition that response to.

At first, there hasn't been any conditioning, although the dogs are very keen to be fed. At this point, the food is called the unconditioned stimulus (UCS) and the salivation is the unconditioned response (UCR) meaning the dogs don't need to be conditioned to drool around tasty food! The footsteps are a neutral stimulus (NS) because, initially, the dogs have no particular interest in the sound.

Step two – the conditioning process

By repeatedly pairing the footsteps with the food, the dogs begin to associate the two and start to link the two stimuli inextricably. At this point, the footsteps have become a conditioned stimulus (CS); the conditioning has linked the sound with food.

Step three – conditioning is complete

Eventually, the dogs begin to salivate when the footsteps are presented without the food. They have developed a conditioned response (CR) to them.

In this example, Pavlov paired the UCS with something pleasant. Aversion therapy pairs unwanted behaviour like smoking with something unpleasant, so it works the other way. This is sometimes called 'counter-conditioning'. Pairing the act of smoking with unpleasant odours, nausea or electric shocks creates a CR to avoid smoking at all costs.

Of course, clients tend to come with positive conditioned responses to smoking already in place, unlike Pavlov's dogs, who were initially indifferent to the sound of footsteps. This is why we have to make the aversion so powerful that prior associations with smoking are overwhelmed.

Operant conditioning

Operant conditioning is concerned with the consequences of a voluntary behaviour carried out by the subject: in other words, it's about what happens after a behaviour is carried out rather than the behaviour becoming associated with things that happen at the same time. This process is called reinforcement.

Positive reinforcement

If carrying out a behaviour results in pleasurable or desirable consequences, it is being positively reinforced. For example, if a rat in a laboratory cage accidentally pushes a lever and a moment or two later a food treat is dropped into the cage, it is positively reinforced to press the lever again, especially when it's hungry.

Negative reinforcement

If failing to carry out a behaviour results in unpleasant or undesirable consequences, the behaviour is being negatively reinforced. For example, if a rat in a laboratory cage fails to press a lever at least once a minute he gets an electric shock, so he's likely to drop whatever else he's doing and press that lever every fifty-nine seconds for as long as conditions remain unchanged.

Punishment

Where negative reinforcement aims to make a behaviour more likely by imposing penalties if it doesn't happen, punishment seeks to reduce the likelihood of a behaviour by imposing penalties if it does. If our rat, for example, gets an electric shock every time he presses the lever, he'll stop doing it. What punishment fails to do is to replace the unwanted behaviour with anything else, the rat can bimble around the cage and do anything he likes, except pressing the lever, without consequence.

Simply put, punishment is 'Don't do that!' where negative reinforcement is 'Do that or else!'

The majority of researchers consider aversion therapy to be closest to classical conditioning. This is because the unpleasant experiences like nausea or electric shocks are generally paired with the act of smoking to make the whole idea abhorrent.

However, you could also make a case that operant conditioning plays a part, by both negative reinforcement and punishment, depending on your approach and the timing of the aversive stimuli. And if you include suggestions that a sense of freedom and wellbeing will follow the action of rejecting a cigarette, you are also using positive reinforcement.

Appendix Three: reflective practice

Remember that this contains Data Protection-sensitive material and should be stored appropriately. It can be useful to keep a copy of all pro-formas together, separately from client records and filed by presenting issue, so you can leaf through them for ideas without having to go through many client records. This information is available from the website as a downloadable form to print and use in your practice, and you can find out from Appendix One how to access it. If you prefer to create your own, this is the information I suggest you include:

Factual information

- Therapist's name
- Client's name or reference number
- Presenting issue
- Date of first session
- Date of final session
- Total number of sessions
- Did any other issues arise?
- Did you work with these? (If yes, complete a separate pro-forma for each)
- Observable/reported information: for each of the main elements/symptoms of the presenting issue give an estimated percentage improvement, and note if this was your perception or the clients.

Your perceptions and learning

On a scale of one to ten, how well did you get into the client's world?

If your score is less than ten how could it have been improved?

Was your choice of techniques dictated solely by the client's needs?

If no, what else affected it?
How could you prevent this happening again?

Do you think therapy was affected by transference or counter-transference?
If so, how did this manifest itself?
How did you deal with it?
If it caused problems, how can you prevent them from occurring again?

Has this client made you aware of any learning points to take forward to other clients?
If yes, how will you apply these in the future?

Has this client helped you to identify a need for further training or support?
If yes, what do you need?
How and when will you get it?

Any other comments/feedback?

Appendix Four: permission for sharing client's information

This is available from the website as a downloadable resource

[Your practice details]

Client's name **Date of birth**
Address

Therapist's details: as above
To: [Doctor/other professional's name and address]

In accordance with the GDPR Right to Portability, I give permission for [your practice name] to communicate with, contact and share any personal information held about me with the above-named doctor or other professional in connection with my care.

In accordance with the GDPR Right to Portability, I give permission for the above-named doctor or other professional to communicate with, contact and share personal information held about me with [your practice name] in connection with my care, including but not limited to revealing information held in my medical, and if applicable, mental health records.

Statement of Consent:

I understand that personal information is held about me by both parties.

I understand the implications of sharing or not sharing information about me.

I understand that this permission is given entirely voluntarily, and that I can revoke it at any time by notifying the parties above in writing.

Client's Signature
Date

Citations

Introduction

Muppet Wiki. (2020). Lady Holiday | Muppet Wiki | Fandom. [ONLINE] Available at: https://muppet.fandom.com/wiki/Lady_Holiday. [Accessed 11 April 2020].

Jaloba, A., (2014). The Hypnotherapy Handbook. Createspace Independent Publishing Platform.

Brown, J. E. (1997). The question cube: a model for developing question repertoire in training couple and family therapists. *Journal of Marital and Family Therapy, 23*(1), 27–40

Waller, D., (2016). Their Worlds, Your Words: the hypnotherapist's guide to effective scripts and sessions. 1st ed. UK: Ann Jaloba Publishing.

The Therapy Loop

Nuland, William & Field, Peter B. (1970) Smoking and hypnosis: A systematic clinical approach, International Journal of Clinical and Experimental Hypnosis, 18:4, 290-306, DOI: cited on https://www.tandfonline.com/doi/abs/10.1080/00207147008415930 [Accessed 11 April 2020].

All Therapy Loop diagrams included in this book are created by and copyright to David Waller (2020).

Managing client expectations

Jaloba, A., 2014. *First days: how to build a therapy business and stay sane*. 1st ed. UK: CreateSpace Independent Publishing Platform.

Ekberg S., Barnes R. K., Kessler D. S., Malpass A., Shaw A. R. Managing clients' expectations at the outset of online Cognitive Behavioural Therapy (CBT) for depression.

Health Expect. 2016 Jun;19(3):557-69. doi: 10.1111/hex.12227. Epub 2014 Aug 2. PMID: 25088009; PMCID: PMC5055246.

Ekberg, S., Barnes, R. K., Kessler, D. S., Mirza, S., Montgomery, A. A., Malpass, A. and Shaw, A. R. G. (2015) "Relationship between Expectation Management and Client Retention in Online Cognitive Behavioural Therapy," *Behavioural and Cognitive Psychotherapy*. Cambridge University Press, 43(6), pp. 732–743. doi: 10.1017/S1352465814000241.

Working with non-visual clients

www.goodreads.com. (n.d.). *A quote by Eleanor Roosevelt.* [online] Available at: https://www.goodreads.com/quotes/25106-do-one-thing-every-day-that-scares-you [Accessed 1 Jun. 2020].

Lexico Dictionaries | English. (n.d.). *Aphantasia | Definition of Aphantasia by Lexico.* [online] Available at: https://www.lexico.com/en/definition/aphantasia [Accessed 4 May 2020].

www.quora.com. (n.d.). *Is aphantasia linked to any other neurogical or psychological disorders? - Quora.* [online] Available at: https://www.quora.com/Is-aphantasia-linked-to-any-other-neurogical-or-psychological-disorders [Accessed 4 May 2020].

psychclassics.yorku.ca. (n.d.). *Classics in the History of Psychology -- Galton (1880).* [online] Available at: http://psychclassics.yorku.ca/Galton/imagery.htm [Accessed 4 May 2020].

Zeman, A., Dewar, M. & Della Sala, S. (2015). Lives without imagery – Congenital aphantasia. *Cortex*, 73, pp.378–380.

Zeman, A. Z., Della Sala, S., Torrens, L. A., Gountouna, V. E., McGonigle, D. J., & Logie, R. H. (2010). Loss of imagery phenomenology with intact visuo-spatial task performance: a case of 'blind imagination'. Neuropsychologia, 48, 145-155.

Zeman, A., Dewar, M. and Della Sala, S. (2015). Lives without imagery – Congenital aphantasia. *Cortex*, 73, pp.378–380.

Forum discussion (2019). *Is there a cure for aphantasia?* [online] The Aphantasia Network. Available at: https://aphantasia.com/discussion/is-there-a-cure-for-aphantasia/ [Accessed 4 May 2020].

Shank, A. & McDowell, P. (2017.). *Treatment of Aphantasia: Can we Reopen the "Mind's Eye?"* [online] Available at: https://www.aaopt.org/docs/default-document-library/treatment-of-aphantasia.pdf [Accessed 4 May 2020].

Clemens, A. (2018). *When the Mind's Eye Is Blind.* [online] Scientific American. Available at: https://www.scientificamerican.com/article/when-the-minds-eye-is-blind1/.[Accessed 4 May 2020].

Maddox, L. (2019). *Aphantasia: life with no mind's eye.* [online] BBC Science Focus Magazine. Available at: https://www.sciencefocus.com/the-human-body/aphantasia-life-with-no-minds-eye/. [Accessed 4 May 2020].

Hurlburt, R. T. & Schwitzgebel, E. (2007). Describing Inner Experience: proponent meets sceptic. Cambridge, Massachusets: MIT Press.

Kavanagh, A. (2018). *Aphantasia is not a disability.* [online] Medium. Available at: https://medium.com/@artkavanagh/aphantasia-is-not-a-disability-511989fa1e71 [Accessed 4 May 2020].

ibid.

Zeman, A., Dewar, M. & Della Sala, S. (2015). Lives without imagery – Congenital aphantasia. *Cortex*, 73, pp.378–380.

Sigal, Nili. (2018) Extreme Imagination Therapy workshop [online] Available at: http://sites.exeter.ac.uk/eyesmind/files/2018/11/Extreme-Imagination-N-Sigal.pdf [Accessed 4 May 2020].

Silence in therapy

Smith, Andy (2011). *NLP Presuppositions (9): You cannot not communicate*. [online] Practical NLP. Available at: https://nlppod.com/nlp-presuppositions-9-you-cannot-not-communicate/. [Accessed 24 April 2020].

Sharpley, Professor Christopher F., Munro, David M. & Elly, Martin J. (2005) Silence and rapport during initial interviews, Counselling Psychology Quarterly, 18:2, 149-159, DOI: 10.1080/09515070500142189

Lane, R.C., Koetting, M.G. and Bishop, J. (2002). Silence as communication in psychodynamic psychotherapy. *Clinical Psychology Review*, 22(7), pp.1091–1104.

The first six items in this list are based upon: Lane, R.C., Koetting, M.G. and Bishop, J. (2002). Silence as communication in psychodynamic psychotherapy. *Clinical Psychology Review*, 22(7), p 1097-1098.

Self-disclosure

Erickson, M. H. (1959). Further Clinical Techniques of Hypnosis: Utilization Techniques. *American Journal of Clinical Hypnosis*, 2(1), pp.3–21

Pinto-Coelho, K. G., Hill, C. E., Kearney, M. S., Sarno, E. L., Sauber, E. S., Baker, S. M., Brady, J., Ireland, G. W., Hoffman, M. A., Spangler, P. T., & Thompson, B. J. (2018). When in doubt, sit quietly: A qualitative investigation of experienced therapists' perceptions of self-disclosure. *Journal of Counseling Psychology, 65*(4), 440–452. https://doi.org/10.1037/cou0000288 [Accessed 21 February 2020]

Spinelli, E. (2002). On disclosure. In S. du Plock (Ed.) Further existential challenges to psychotherapeutic theory and practice (pp.52–67). London: Society for Existential Analysis. cited in McBeath, Alistair (2015) 'Therapist Self-Disclosure' https://thepsychologist.bps.org.uk/volume-28/july-2015/therapist-self-disclosure [Accessed 21 February 2020]

Counselling Tutor (2016). *Use of Self in Counselling • Counselling Tutor*. [online] Counselling Tutor. Available at: https://counsellingtutor.com/use-of-self-in-counselling/. [Accessed 6 June 2020].

Ferraro, Josephine (2010) 'How psychotherapists' self-disclosure affects the therapeutic relationship with clients' http://psychotherapist-nyc.blogspot.com/2010/06/how-psychotherapists-self-disclosure.html [Accessed 21 February 2020]

Opencolleges.edu.au. (2016). *5 Golden Rules for Using Self-Disclosure in Counselling | Open Colleges*. [online] Available at: https://www.opencolleges.edu.au/careers/blog/self-disclosure-in-counselling. [Accessed 22 February 2020]

Aversion therapy

Butler, Alia. (2015) 'Aversion Therapy and Smoking'. *Livestrong.com* http://www.livestrong.com/article/131926-aversion-therapy-smoking/. [Accessed 7 December 2015]

Hajek, P. & Stead L. F. 'Aversive smoking for smoking cessation.' *Cochrane Database of Systematic Reviews* 2001, Issue 3. Art. No.: CD000546. DOI: 10.1002/14651858.CD000546.pub2. http://www.ncsct.co.uk/usr/pub/aversive-smoking-for-smoking-cessation.pdf. [Accessed 7 December 2015]

ibid. p3-4

Barber, Nigel (2010) 'Smoking: Most effective quitting technique little known.' *Psychology Today blog* https://www.psychologytoday.com/blog/the-human-beast/201002/smoking-most-effective-quitting-technique-little-known. [Accessed 7 December 2015]

cited on http://addictionrehabnow.com/acupuncture-hypnosis-helps-quitting/, [accessed Dec. 2015]

Hajek P. & Stead L. F. 'Aversive smoking for smoking cessation.' *Cochrane Database of Systematic Reviews* 2001, Issue 3. page 6. Art. No.: CD000546. DOI: 10.1002/14651858.CD000546.pub2. http://www.ncsct.co.uk/usr/pub/aversive-smoking-for-smoking-cessation.pdf. [Accessed & December 2015]

Dinh-Williams, Laurence, Mendrek, Adrianna, Bourque, Josiane, & Potvin, Stéphane (2014) "Where there's smoke, there's fire: The brain reactivity of chronic smokers when exposed to the negative value of smoking." *Progress in Neuro-Psychopharmacology and Biological Psychiatry* Volume 50, 3 April 2014, Pages 66–73 http://www.sciencedirect.com/science/article/pii/S0278584613002881 [Accessed 7 December 2015]

Effective Client notes

Complementary and Natural Healthcare Council. (2014). Code of Conduct, Ethics, and Performance, as updated 1 June 2018, paragraph B7. [ONLINE] Available at: https://www.cnhc.org.uk/sites/default/files/Downloads/CodeofConductEthicsandPerformance.pdf. [Accessed 8 April 2020]

Reflective practice

Bennett-Levy, J., Thwaites, R., Chaddock, A. & Davis, M. (2009). Reflective practice in cognitive behavioural therapy: The engine of lifelong learning. [online] Available at: https://pdfs.semanticscholar.org/cc66/1f7c88a48c6a5b80002923a2760d99d0802b.pdf. [Accessed 17 January 2020].

Mearns, D. (1997). *Person-Centred Counselling Training*. London: Sage pp88-89, cited on Counsellor London | Psychotherapy London | The Fleet Street Practice| Annette Ansell Counsellor. 2020. Supervision of counsellors and Therapists. [ONLINE] Available at: http://www.londoncounsellor.org.uk/supervision. [Accessed 9 April 2020].

Displaying prices

Inspiration Center - Business, Website and Marketing Inspiration. (2020). The Difference Between Value and Cost, and How it Will Crush Your Sales if You Get it Wrong. [ONLINE] Available at: https://www.weebly.com/inspiration/difference-between-value-and-cost. [Accessed 9 April 2020].

Networking

Cambridge English Dictionary. (2020). NETWORKING | meaning in the Cambridge English Dictionary. [ONLINE] Available at: https://dictionary.cambridge.org/dictionary/english/networking. [Accessed 9 April 2020].

Psychology Today. (2020). The Water Cooler Effect | Psychology Today. [ONLINE] Available at: https://www.psychologytoday.com/us/blog/reality-mining/200911/the-water-cooler-effect. [Accessed 9 April 2020].

Wikipedia. (2020). Pareto principle - Wikipedia. [ONLINE] Available at: https://en.wikipedia.org/wiki/Pareto_principle. [Accessed 10 April 2020].

Word of mouth referrals

Khalid Saleh. (2020). The Importance of Word of Mouth Marketing – Statistics and Trends. [ONLINE] Available at: https://www.invespcro.com/blog/word-of-mouth-marketing. [Accessed 10 April 2020].

Sukhraj, Ramona. (2018). 7 Must-Have Word-of-Mouth Marketing Strategies [Infographic]. [ONLINE] Available at: https://www.impactbnd.com/blog/word-of-mouth-marketing-strategies-infographic. [Accessed 10 April 2020].

Whitler, Kimberly A.. (2014). Why Word of Mouth Marketing is the Most Important Social Media. [ONLINE] Available at: https://www.forbes.com/sites/kimberlywhitler/2014/07/17/why-word-of-mouth-marketing-is-the-most-important-social-media/#170172054a8c. [Accessed 10 April 2020].

Blogging

Schäferhoff, Nick. (2018). What is the Optimal Content Length? - Here's What the Science Says. [ONLINE] Available at: https://torquemag.io/2018/04/optimal-content-length. [Accessed 10 April 2020].

Contraindications and medical referrals

The General Hypnotherapy Register's Code of Ethics. (2020). The General Hypnotherapy Register's Code of Ethics. [ONLINE] Available at: https://www.general-hypnotherapy-register.com/code-of-ethics. [Accessed 5 April 2020].

CNHC. (2020). Homepage | CNHC. [ONLINE] Available at: https://www.cnhc.org.uk. [Accessed 5 April 2020].

Complementary and Natural Healthcare Council. (2017, amended 2019). Core Curriculum for Hypnotherapy. [ONLINE] Available at: https://www.cnhc.org.uk/sites/default/files/Downloads/Hypnotherapy-core-curriculum.pdf. [Accessed 5 April 2020].

Ibid.

Advertising Standards Authority | Committee of Advertising Practice. (2020). Home - ASA | CAP. [ONLINE] Available at: https://www.asa.org.uk. [Accessed 5 April 2020].

Advertising Standards Authority | Committee of Advertising Practice. 2020. Health: Hypnotherapy - ASA | CAP. [ONLINE] Available at: https://www.asa.org.uk/advice-online/health-hypnotherapy.html. [Accessed 5 April 2020].

Advertising Standards Authority | Committee of Advertising Practice. 2020. Legislation - ASA | CAP. [ONLINE] Available at: https://www.asa.org.uk/advice-online/legislation.html. [Accessed 8 April 2020].

Paradoxical anxiety

NBC News. (2020). Chilling out no help for those with relaxation-induced anxiety. [ONLINE] Available at: https://www.nbcnews.com/health/body-odd/chilling-out-no-help-those-relaxation-induced-anxiety-flna1C7569380. [Accessed 05 April 2020].

ScienceDaily. (2020). People with anxiety may strategically choose worrying over relaxing -- ScienceDaily. [ONLINE] Available at: https://www.sciencedaily.com/releases/2019/09/190930114737.htm. [Accessed 05 April 2020].

Berman, R & D'Emilio, G. (2019). Relaxation makes worriers more anxious. [ONLINE] Available at: https://www.medicalnewstoday.com/articles/326646.php#1. [Accessed 05 April 2020].

Newman M. G., Lafreniere L. S., Jacobson N. C. Relaxation-induced anxiety: Effects of peak and trajectories of change on treatment outcome for generalized anxiety disorder. Psychother Res. 2018 Jul;28(4):616-629. doi: 10.1080/10503307.2016.1253891. Epub 2016 Nov 18. PMID: 27855541; PMCID: PMC6134846. [Accessed 05 April 2020].

Mental Health Daily. (2020). Relaxation-Induced Anxiety: Potential Causes & Solutions - Mental Health Daily. [ONLINE] Available at: https://mentalhealthdaily.com/2015/03/15/relaxation-induced-anxiety-potential-causes-solutions/. [Accessed 05 April 2020].

Learned helplessness

Diagram originally published in Spielman, Rose M., Dumper, Kathryn, Jenkins, William, Lacombe, Arlene, Lovett, Marilyn,

& Perlmutter, Marion. (2014). Psychology. OpenStax: Houston, Texas. Available for free at https://openstax.org/books/psychology/pages/1-introduction [accessed 1.12.20]

Seligman, M. E. P. (1972). "Learned helplessness". Annual Review of Medicine. 23 (1): 407–412.

Lack of progress

Pearson, J. E. (2007) Hypnotizability - Do You Have It? [ONLINE] Available at: http://EzineArticles.com/459700. [Accessed 05 April 2020].

Clients who don't show up

GoodTherapy.org Therapy Blog. (2013). Why Do People Leave Therapy Prematurely?. [ONLINE] Available at: https://www.goodtherapy.org/blog/why-do-clients-leave-therapy-prematurely-0627137. [Accessed 5 April 2020].

Sims, H. et al (2012) *Text Message Reminders of Appointments: A Pilot Intervention at Four Community Mental Health Clinics in London*, cited on Psychiatry Online. 2020. Psychiatry Online. [ONLINE] Available at: http://ps.psychiatryonline.org/doi/abs/10.1176/appi.ps.201100211. [Accessed 4 April 2020]

Problems with payments

Lovetts Solicitors. (2020). Letter Before Action. [ONLINE] Available at: https://lovetts.co.uk/uk-debt-recovery/letter-before-action. [Accessed 4 April 2020].

Difficult clients

Dangeli, Jevon. (2020). The Presuppositions of NLP | Jevon Dangeli.com. [ONLINE] Available at:

https://jevondangeli.com/the-presuppositions-of-nlp-2. [Accessed 5 April 2020].

van de Snepscheut, Jan L. A. (2020). Wikiquote. [ONLINE] Available at: https://en.wikiquote.org/wiki/Jan_L._A._van_de_Snepscheut. [Accessed 6 April 2020].

Kazantzis, N., Whittington, C., & Dattilio, F. (2010). Meta-analysis of homework effects in cognitive and behavioral therapy: A replication and extension. Clinical Psychology: Science and Practice, 17(2), 144-156.

Thase, Michael & Callan, Judith. (2006). The role of homework in cognitive behavior therapy of depression. Journal of Psychotherapy Integration. 16. 162-177. 10.1037/1053-0479.16.2.162.

Therapist Aid. (n.d.). *Successful Therapy Termination (Guide).* [online] Available at: https://www.therapistaid.com/therapy-guide/successful-therapy-termination#:~:text=Some%20clients%20may%20be%20reluctant [Accessed 3 June 2020].

Complementary and Natural Healthcare Council. (2019). Guidance to the Duty of Candour. [ONLINE] Available at: https://www.cnhc.org.uk/sites/default/files/Downloads/CNHC%20Candour%20Guidance%20July%202019.pdf. [Accessed 5 April 2020].

Getting the most from supervision

General Hypnotherapy Standards Council & General Hypnotherapy Register. (2020). Supervision & CPD

Policy. [ONLINE] Available at: https://www.general-hypnotherapy-register.com/supervision-cpd-policy. [Accessed 15 March 2020].

CounsellingResource.com: Psychology, Therapy & Mental Health Resources. (2020). Supervision in Counselling and Therapy. [ONLINE] Available at: http://counsellingresource.com/lib/therapy/aboutcouns/supervision. [Accessed 15 March 2020].

Proctor, B. (1996) Clinical Supervision in Practice: A Working Model As cited on www.supervision&coaching.com. [Accessed 10 October 2016]

Gallon, S. (2002) *Clinical Supervision Training Manual*. Portland, OR: Northwest Frontier ATTC.

London Deanery. (2012). What is Supervision For? [ONLINE] Available at: http://www.faculty.londondeanery.ac.uk/e-learning/supervision/what-is-supervision-for. [Accessed 3 December 2017].

Wallbank, Sonya & Hatton, Sue. 'Reducing burnout and stress: the effectiveness of clinical supervision'. in *Community Practitioner*, 84(7), July 2011, pp 31-35. Community Practitioners' and Health Visitors' Association

SurveyMonkey. (2015). Hypnotherapy Supervision Survey [ONLINE] Available at: https://www.surveymonkey.com/results/SM-5ZLZJTSY. [Accessed 15 March 2020].

Compassion Fatigue

Kearney M. K., Weininger R. B., Vachon M. L. S., et al. Self-care of physicians caring for patients at the end of life: 'Being connected ... a key to my survival.' *JAMA* 2009; 301:1,155-1,164. Cited in (2009). *What is burnout vs. compassion fatigue?* [online] Relias Media. Available at: https://www.reliasmedia.com/articles/113896-what-is-burnout-vs-compassion-fatigue. [Accessed 11 May 2020].

Portnoy, D. (2011). *Burnout And Compassion Fatigue: Watch For The Signs* in Health Progress July - August 2011 pp. 46-50 [online] Compassion Fatigue Awareness Project. Available at: http://www.compassionfatigue.org/pages/healthprogress.pdf. [Accessed 11 May 2020].

Wikipedia Contributors (2019). *Compassion fatigue*. [online] Wikipedia. Available at: https://en.wikipedia.org/wiki/Compassion_fatigue. [Accessed 11 May 2020].

Questions from the front line

Encyclopedia Britannica. (n.d.). *George A. Miller | American psychologist*. [online] Available at: https://www.britannica.com/biography/George-A-Miller#ref1200618. [Accessed 22 May 2020].

Overview - TOTE Quick reference. (n.d.). [online] Oxford Reference. Available at: https://www.oxfordreference.com/view/10.1093/oi/authority.20110803105039783. [Accessed 22 May 2020].

Schetky MD, D. (2001). *On treating two members of the same family*. [online] American Academy of Child and Adolescent Psychiatry. Available at: https://www.aacap.org/App_Themes/AACAP/docs/member_resources/ethics/in_action/columns/on_treating_two_members_of_the_same_family.pdf. [Accessed 18 May 2020].

National Council for Hypnotherapy. (2017). *Code of Conduct - National Council for Hypnotherapy*. [online] Available at: https://www.hypnotherapists.org.uk/about-nch/code-of-ethics. [Accessed 23 May 2020].

General Hypnotherapy Register (2020). *The General Hypnotherapy Register's Code of Ethics*. [online] Available at: https://www.general-hypnotherapy-register.com/code-of-ethics. [Accessed 23 May 2020].

Legislation.gov.uk. (2010). *Equality Act 2010*. [online] Available at: http://www.legislation.gov.uk/ukpga/2010/15/contents, with explanatory notes at http://www.legislation.gov.uk/ukpga/2010/15/notes/contents. [Accessed 18 May 2020].

Ibid.

Fair Play For Women. (2018). *The Equality Act 2010: A woman's right to single-sex spaces*. [online] Available at: https://fairplayforwomen.com/equality-act-2010_womens-rights/#jump1. [Accessed 19 May 2020].

Citizens Advice. (2020). Single-sex and separate services for men and women. [ONLINE] Available at: https://www.citizensadvice.org.uk/consumer/discrimination-in-the-provision-of-goods-and-services/discrimination-in-the-provision-of-goods-and-services1/goods-and-services-what-are-the-different-types-of-discrimination/what-doesn-t-count-as-unlawful-discrimination-in-goods-and-services/single-sex-and-separate-services-for-men-and-women-when-discrimination-is-allowed. [Accessed 19 May 2020].

Equality and Human Rights Commission. (2018) What equality law means for your business. Page 17. [online] Available at: https://www.equalityhumanrights.com/sites/default/

files/what-equality-law-means-for-your-business-2018.pdf. [Accessed 23 May 2020].

Sensitive Therapist. (n.d.). *How Many Clients Can I See Before I Get Burned Out?* [online] Available at: https://www.sensitivetherapist.com/blog/how-many-clients. [Accessed 22 May 2020].

Newswise.com. (2004) Southern Connecticut State University. *Caseload of Therapist a Major Factor in Treating Depression*. [online] Available at: https://www.newswise.com/articles/caseload-of-therapist-a-major-factor-in-treating-depression. [Accessed 22 May 2020].

Wikipedia. (2020). Plate spinning - Wikipedia. [ONLINE] Available at: https://en.wikipedia.org/wiki/Plate_spinning. [Accessed 25 March 2020].

Businessnewsdaily.com. (2020). *Do You Have a Healthy Work-Life Balance?* [online] Available at: https://www.businessnewsdaily.com/8108-work-life-balance-quiz.html. [Accessed 22 May 2020]. Quiz used here with permission from Joanie Connell PhD of Flexible Work Solutions: Lessons from the Workplace. (n.d.). *Lessons from the Workplace*. [online] Available at: https://flexibleworksolutions.com. [Accessed 22 May 2020]

Selftherapyjourney.com. (n.d.). *Description of the Self-Care Capacity*. [online] Available at: https://selftherapyjourney.com/Pattern/Description/Self_Care_Capacity_Description_Beginning.aspx. [Accessed 23 May 2020].

Pahr, K. (2018). *For Many People with Anxiety, Self-Care Just Doesn't Work*. [online] Healthline. Available at: https://www.healthline.com/health/mental-health/self-care-is-hard#3. [Accessed 23 May 2020].

Ibid.

Bloom, P. (2016). *Against Empathy: The Case for Rational Compassion*. 1st ed. Ecco. cited in Carter, J. (2018). *The Dangers of Being an Empathetic Leader*. [Online] Entrepreneur. Available at: https://www.entrepreneur.com/article/311413. [Accessed 23 May 2020].

Psychiatry & Psychotherapy Podcast. (2019). *How Empathy Works and How To Improve It*. [online] Available at: https://psychiatrypodcast.com/psychiatry-psychotherapy-podcast/how-empathy-works-and-how-to-improve-it. [Accessed 23 May 2020].

Kalavana, T.V. (2018). *Finding the Right Level of Empathy in Business Leadership*. [online] Chief Learning Officer - CLO Media. Available at: https://www.chieflearningofficer.com/2018/03/15/finding-right-level-empathy. [Accessed 23 May 2020].

Appendix Two: behavioural conditioning

McLeod, S. A. (2018, October 08). *Pavlov's dogs*. Simply Psychology. https://www.simplypsychology.org/pavlov.html. [Accessed 5 June 2020].

Cherry, K. (2005). *What Is Operant Conditioning and How Does It Work?* [online] Verywell Mind. Available at: https://www.verywellmind.com/operant-conditioning-a2-2794863. [Accessed 5 June 2020].

The Psychology Notes Headquarters. (2012). *Aversion Therapy*. [online] Available at: https://www.psychologynoteshq.com/aversiontherapy. [Accessed 5 Jun. 2020].

Staff, T. (2018). *Everything You Need To Know About Aversion Therapy*. [online] Thrivetalk. Available at: https://www.thrivetalk.com/aversion-therapy. [Accessed 5 June 2020].

Additional references

Additional references

American Psychological Association. 2020. Old problem, new tools. [ONLINE] Available at: https://www.apa.org/monitor/2009/10/helplessness. [Accessed 05 April 2020].

Batson, J. (2011). *Compassion Fatigue - The American Institute of Stress*. [online] The American Institute of Stress. Available at: https://www.stress.org/military/forpractitionersleaders/compassion-fatigue. [Accessed 11 May 2020].

Bray, Bethany. (2019) 'Counselor self-disclosure: encouragement or impediment to client growth?' https://ct.counseling.org/2019/01/counselor-selfdisclosure-encouragement-or-impediment-to-clientgrowth/ [Accessed 21.2.2020]

Franklin, Shelby (2017). *5 types of self-care for your Mental Health*. [online] The Mighty. Available at: https://themighty.com/2017/11/types-of-self-care-formental-health/. [Accessed 21.2.2020]

Google Books. (2020) Social Psychology, 2nd Edition – Roger Brown - Google Books. [ONLINE] Available at: https://buff.ly/3kWxigV. [Accessed 05 April 2020].

Google Books. (2020) Theories of Human Development – Barbara M. Newman, Philip R. Newman - Google Books. [ONLINE] Available at: https://buff.ly/3nQYpvU[Accessed 05 April 2020]

Kazantzis, N., Whittington, C., & Dattilio, F. (2010). Meta-analysis of homework effects in cognitive and behavioral therapy: A replication and extension.

Clinical Psychology: Science and Practice, 17(2), 144-156.

Kent. Rosemary. (2017) C4 information sheet What do counsellors and psychotherapists mean by "professional boundaries". [online] Available at: https://www.bacp.co.uk/media/2638/bacp-whattherapists-mean-by-professional-boundaries-c4.pdf. [Accessed 21.2.2020].

London Hypnotherapy (n.d.) 'What is Rogerian Therapy?' Available at: http://www.londonhypnotherapyuk.com/what-is-rogerian-psychotherapy/ [Accessed 21.2.2020]

Medical News Today. (2020) Learned helplessness: Examples, symptoms, and treatment. [ONLINE] Available at: https://www.medicalnewstoday.com/articles/325355.php#in-adults. [Accessed 05 April 2020].

Mindtools.com. (2019). *Empathy at Work: Developing Skills to Understand Other People*. [online] Available at: https://www.mindtools.com/pages/article/EmpathyatWork.htm. [Accessed 06 April 2020].

Moulder, H., J. D.. and A. C. C. (2019). *Why You Feel Guilty About Taking Care Of Yourself [And What To Do]*. [online] Course Correction Coaching | Heather Moulder. Available at: https://www.coursecorrectioncoaching.com/guiltytaking-care-of-yourself/. [Accessed 06 April 2020].

Shetky MD, D. (2001). On treating two members of the same family. [online] American Academy of Child and Adolescent Psychiatry. Available at: https://buff.ly/3fuclsG [Accessed 18 May 2020].

Stern, Robin & Divecha, Diana. (2015). *How to Avoid the Empathy Trap*. [online] Available at:

https://greatergood.berkeley.edu/article/item/how_to _avoid_the_empathy_trap. {Accessed 03 April 2020].

Turner, Jessica N. (2005). *Selfcare versus Guilt - Propel Women*. [online] Available at: https://www.propelwomen.org/content/selfcareversus -guilt/gjeb1r?permcode=gjeb1r. [Accessed 05 April 2020].

Wikipedia. (2020). *Compassion fatigue*. [online] Available at: https://en.wikipedia.org/wiki/Compassion_fatigue#Fac tors_contributing_to_compassion_fatigue_in_student_ affairs_professionals [Accessed 11 May 2020].

Zur, Ofer. Self-disclosure and transparency in psychotherapy and counselling, https://www.zurinstitute.com/selfdisclosure-1/ [accessed 21 February 2020]

Index

Printed in Great Britain
by Amazon

67047991R00138